SpringerBriefs in Ethics

More information about this series at http://www.springer.com/series/10184

Maria Bonnafous-Boucher • Jacob Dahl Rendtorff

Stakeholder Theory

A Model for Strategic Management

 Springer

Maria Bonnafous-Boucher
Full Professor Paris Chamber of Commerce
    and Industry
Paris, France

Jacob Dahl Rendtorff
Roskilde University
Roskilde, Denmark

Translated by Michael Lavin

ISSN 2211-8101
SpringerBriefs in Ethics
ISBN 978-3-319-44355-3
DOI 10.1007/978-3-319-44356-0

ISSN 2211-811X   (electronic)

ISBN 978-3-319-44356-0   (eBook)

Library of Congress Control Number: 2016956693

Printed on acid-free paper

This Springer imprint is published by Springer Nature
The registered company is Springer International Publishing AG Switzerland

Preface

It is a special pleasure and privilege to write this preface to Stakeholder Theory. A Model for Strategic Management. While much of this book is territory that is familiar to me, there is much new ground. They have built on the contributions of many others, and suggested that stakeholder theory can be pushed in new directions that are important to make societies better.

When they suggest that "Stakeholder theory examines the displacement of traditional sovereignties towards other forms of institutional legitimacy" they rightly understand the critical philosophical attitude which comprise the origins of the theory from Rhenman onwards. Their conclusion is equally powerful:

> In the final analysis, stakeholder theory questions the traditional frontiers between the public space and the private space; it deconstructs the categories of political philosophy, ethics, the economy of organizations, and corporate strategy; it suggests treating these categories in a new way. It borrows the most classical concepts from currents of liberal philosophy from Locke to Rawls in order to them in contemporary forms of sovereignty, of government, of civil society, of social contract, of the redefinition of the common good, of social justice, of deliberation in the public space. In so doing, stakeholder theory creates a current within contemporary political philosophy, that of a critical philosophy of institutions, particularly the corporation.

Seeing the development of stakeholder theory as a way to set business within society, rather than in some fictional space of abstract economics or "free markets disconnected with the humanness of real business" is an achievement of the first order.

It is my sincere hope that this book catalyzes a line of research that connects business theory with political philosophy. For too long business theory has been separated from the rest of the human sciences, especially those who recognize the normative as fundamental. And equally, for too long the first question of political philosophy has been, "how is the state to be justified". Stakeholder theory as interpreted in this volume has the potential to build more useful theories about the connections between business and political life, between business theory and political philosophy and ethics, and between the practical worlds of business and civil society. Such as task may turn out to be central to building a world that is worth leaving to our children.

University Professor   R. Edward Freeman
The Darden School
University of Virginia
Charlottesville, VA, USA
December, 2012

Acknowledgments

As the main contributor, I would like to take this opportunity to thank everyone who helped to make this book possible, especially my coauthor, Jacob Dahl Rendtorff. I would also like to thank Thomas Donaldson, the professors at the Legal Studies and Business Ethics Department at Wharton, as well as Albert David, Julie Battilana, Philippe Desbrières, Jean-Pierre Bréchet, Isabelle Huault, Michael Lavin, Hervé Mesure, Arnaud Stimec, Christian Thuderoz, William Zartman, Edward Freeman, and the anonymous reviewers of the "Repères" collection.

Maria Bonnafous-Boucher

Contents

Introduction

Between 1984 and 2012, much has been written and said about stakeholder theory. Published in 2010, R. E. Freeman's *Stakeholder Theory: The State of the Art* provides an overview of the major contributions in the field. The uninterrupted and increasingly rapid flow of publications up until that time attests to the importance of the theory.

This book puts the importance of stakeholder theory into perspective, first as a negotiated model of governance; second, as a descriptive, explicative, and interpretative framework for modalities of decision-making and action in management; and third, as a local theory, developed in the field of strategic management, extending beyond the confines of the discipline in which it originated. The principal objective of this book is to highlight the philosophical (political and moral) issues inherent in a management model.

Stakeholder theory is without doubt a local theory in that the sources of the notion of the stakeholder are to be found in a specific form of organization – the multinational company – in a particular context, the globalized economy of the 1980s and 1990s. Stakeholder theory is concerned with the representation of decision-making mechanisms and power relations within such organizations; it offers a way of reappraising the models of governance of the multinational and, consequently, the possibility of redistributing the wealth it creates taking into account the parties which interact with it directly or exert an influence over it indirectly. Moreover, stakeholder theory reappraises the corporate environment by introducing a series of sometimes converging, but often conflicting, interests; it deepens the notion of the strategic environment by extending the postulate according to which doing business is more than just making money. Consequently, it attempts to better situate the place and role of the corporation in society and to analyze the impacts of its activity on the economic, political, social, legal, cultural, and ecological environment. In short, stakeholder theory reconciles business ethics and strategy.

However, there is no denying that, although anchored in research focusing on corporate life, the notion of the stakeholder is enjoying growing influence beyond the frontiers of management. What, then, is the real scope of the notion and the theory that has emerged from it? Deriving from management, can it impact on other fields of knowledge and other practices? Such a hypothesis may corroborate the idea according to which our systems of thought are fed by a managerial tropism (Gary S. Becker's Foucauldian reading). Is the corporation, now a fundamental economic unit of society, destined to become a fundamental social unit too? Indeed, according to some commentators, the underlying intention of stakeholder theory is to affect this transformation. That is why it is legitimate to ask questions about the extension of the theory beyond the field of management science. However, for good or ill, stakeholder theory rethinks and attempts to resolve, in the sphere of business life, questions as decisive as those concerning the interests of one or more social categories, or even one or more social classes. It appraises the rise – through deliberative and participative practices – of democratic processes in all organizations up to corporate government. It reflects on the concrete consequences that this phenomenon represents for the distribution of powers. It highlights, through the necessary distribution of wealth, the possibility of a form of social justice within the corporation. Lastly, it asks questions about the contribution of commercial firms to the common good of society.

The reader will perhaps find it surprising that a theory and a concept, the sources of which are to be found in management science, can be used to explain situations not limited to either economic or corporate life. This explanatory power, or what we refer to as the heuristic function of the theory, is all the more penetrating in that it is based on a comparison of current perspectives in management studies. Indeed, the fecundity of the theory derives from its local precision, which encourages both critical and constructive studies on democratic mechanisms and corporate governance structures, as well as on organizational systems at the crossroads between private and public life.

Thanks to its heuristic function (Bonnafous-Boucher 2011),[1] the value of stakeholder theory is largely based on its capacity to develop notions which transform our ways of thinking about the organization of power, decision-making, and action. Whence its practical usefulness, which, however, is often called into question. In this book, we propose a normative heuristic approach.

Chapter 1 consists in an examination of the process whereby the notion of the stakeholder became a theory. A number of definitions are addressed, including the now well-established conceptual framework first mooted in the 1960s and developed in the 1980s. This brief panorama provides an outline of the parameters of the theory and contextualizes the epistemological debates that have arisen around it, debates that have led to the development of a kind of theoretical pluralism and to the emergence of a number of critiques. The scope and potential for extending the theory to other fields are also discussed.

Chapter 2 provides a description of the theory's roots in strategic management and outlines how it reflects a historically constructed conception of the corporation that differs from a financial or merely competitive representation of the economic actor in an economic, social, and cultural environment. Stakeholder theory situates

---

[1] The references between brackets refer to the bibliography at the end of the book.

the corporation between a dependence on the environment and the possibility of determining its own policy. Congruent approaches are examined, including the French approach, which identifies the corporation as a political system; the resource- and skills-based approach; and the approach representing the corporation as a network of complex relations.

Chapter 3 deals with stakeholder theory's contribution to organization studies, an aspect ignored by the authors of the theory themselves.

Chapter 4 presents an overview of conflicts over legitimacy between traditional public institutions and international organizations. The possibility or impossibility of constructing a social contract on contemporary foundations is examined, and the links between stakeholder theory and theories of justice and the redistribution of wealth are discussed. As an immediate consequence of these politico-philosophical and moral considerations, stakeholder theory is, in this book, considered not as a marginal approach to social questions affecting the corporation, nor as a kind of borderless actor theory, but as a theory capable of regenerating problematics as fundamental as those of the nature of the corporation and the emergence of a transnational civil society.

Chapter 5 deals with the relationship between stakeholder theory and ethics.

Chapter 1
From "The Stakeholder" to Stakeholder Theory

Definitions

The term stakeholder ("partie prenante" in French) is used in different ways by specialists and members of the public. For the wider public, it is a generic term, equivalent to "citizen," to anyone taking part in public life. For specialists, it refers to people who are not shareholders. In fact, "partie prenante" is an imperfect translation of the English *stakeholder*, literally the "holder" of a "stake." Less literally, *stakeholder* means he, or she, who has a stake in something. More broadly, it means someone who participates or "takes part" in something ("prendre partie," hence "partie prenante"). In English, the term *stakeholder* is a neologism which plays on the term *stockholder* (designating those who share the profits, including the shareholders). The term indicates that parties other than *stockholders* can have a say and that their stakes and interests in the activities of the firm should be recognized (Freeman and Reed 1983). It defines individuals and groups of individuals indispensible to the survival of the firm and who are either consulted or participate directly in decision-making processes or arbitrage. But from which point of view is the question of survival to be considered: from that of the firm or that of the stakeholder? It is for this reason that some Francophone authors prefer the term "partie intéressée" ("interested party") (Benseddik 2006) or "ayant droit" ("rights holder") (Mercier 2006). Perhaps not surprisingly, for the Swedish administrative research school of the 1960s, represented by Rhenman and Stymne (1965), the notion of the stakeholder is seen as reciprocal relationship in which a stakeholder is a group which depends on the firm in order to achieve its own objectives and on which the firm depends for its survival.

Officially, the term "stakeholder" was first used in public at a conference held at the Stanford Research Institute in 1963 to refer to "all groups on which an organization is dependent for its survival." But it was only 20 years later that the term "stakeholder" was popularized by Freeman (1984) who, at that time, used it to mean: "an individual or group of individuals which can affect or be affected by the achievement

© The Author(s) 2016
M. Bonnafous-Boucher, J.D. Rendtorff, *Stakeholder Theory*, SpringerBriefs in Ethics, DOI 10.1007/978-3-319-44356-0_1

of organizational objectives." Only those who cannot affect (due to an incapacity to do so) and those who are not affected by the actions of an organization (due to the absence of any form of relationship) are excluded from this definition. It should also be noted that a stakeholder can be affected by the corporation without being able to affect it in turn (and vice-versa). Potentially, and alternatively, it can contribute to or threaten the organization.

In the final analysis, while the term "stakeholder" is closely associated with the private sector and the corporate world, it is also revealing in terms of the relationship between the business world and public life: it illustrates the difficulty of dissociating various interests, since the environment within which corporations act is not only economic and legal, but also social, political, cultural and ecological. In fact, the term "stakeholder" has crossed the borders of corporate governance and is now frequently used by political analysts, as evidenced by the White Book on European governance (Candela 2006), and by numerous political scientists (Ackerman and Fischkin 2004). Nevertheless, the decision-making processes of national public organizations (states, public authorities), regional public organizations (the European Union), and para-public organizations (associations, international NGOs) has little to do with the corporate governance model.

Consequently, it is difficult to determine *a priori* who is a stakeholder and who or what is not. It depends on a concrete analysis of the precise situation in which an organization or, more specifically, a corporation, finds itself. Whether in public debates or in debates on corporate management, the notion of the stakeholder is generally associated with that of the actor concerned with a decision or a project. It seems to complement the notions of the historical social actor (Bourdieu), the strategic actor (Crozier), the identity-creating actor (Sainsaulieu), the group actor (Kaes, Anzieu), and the impulse actor (Enriquez), a family of concepts traversing many of the social sciences. Stakeholders are constantly implicated in collective, public action in terms of both analysis and practice. It is as if, in order to govern, or quite simply to win agreement to a reform, it is sufficient to be aware of the interests and influence of various groups. Thus, in a neo-liberal context, integrating stakeholders into an action framework takes the form of a pertinent, actionable theory (Audier 2012) in which everything is negotiable in a context in which decisions are made in function of events and their impacts (Bonnafous-Boucher 2004). But who or what is a stakeholder and who isn't? If everything, either in an absolute or relative manner, is a stakeholder, is the fact of acting tantamount merely to establishing degrees of engagement or disengagement? In many regards, stakeholder theory bears witness to a desire for change in approaches to governance, decision-making, acting, feeling or wanting to be part of a project. It reflects a shared aspiration to participate; it highlights the questionable nature of the distinction between those who have rights and those who do not. It takes into account the blind spot constituted by those who do not express an opinion. That is why, although it undeniably derives from management studies, it can also be regarded as a theory critical of neo-liberalism.

In a well known article, Mitchell et al. (1997) attempted to put an end to the debate on the identity of stakeholders once and for all. The authors suggested that the problematic should be reduced to the following question: who really counts for the firm? Clearly, the authors consider stakeholder theory exclusively from the point of view of usefulness to the corporation (Table 1.1).

Table 1.1 What is a "stakeholder"? A chronology

Source	Stake
Stanford memo (1963)	"those groups without whose support the organization would cease to exist" (cited in Freeman and Reed 1983; Freeman 1984)
Rhenman (1964)	"are depending on the firm in order to achieve their personal goals and on whom the firm is depending for its existence"
Ahlstedt and Jahnukainen (1971)	"driven by their own interests and goals are participants in a firm, and thus depending on it and whom for its sake the firm is depending" (cited in Näsi 1995)
Freeman and Reed (1983: 91)	Wide: "can affect the achievement of an organization's objectives or who is affected by the achievement of an organization's objectives"
	Narrow: "on which the organization is dependent for its continued survival"
Freeman (1984: 46)	"can affect or is affected by the achievement of the organization's objectives"
Freeman and Gilbert (1987: 397)	"can affect or is affected by a business"
Cornell and Shapiro (1987: 5)	"claimants" who have "contacts"
Evan and Freeman (1988: 75–76)	"have a stake in or claim on the firm"
Evan and Freeman (1988: 79)	"benefit or are harmed by, and whose rights are violated or respected by, corporate actions"
Bowie (1988a, b: 112, Note 2)	"without whose support the organization would cease to exist"
Alkhafaji (1989: 36)	"groups to whom the corporation is responsible"
Carroll (1989: 57)	"asserts to have one or more of these kinds of stakes" – "ranging from an interest to a right (legal or moral) to ownership or legal title to the company's assets or property"
Evan and Freeman (1990)	contract holders
Thomson et al. (1991: 209)	In "relationship with an organization"
Savage et al. (1991: 61)	"have an interest in the actions of an organization and … the ability to influence it"
Hill and Jones (1992: 133)	"constituents who have a legitimate claim on the firm … established through the existence of an exchange relationship" who supply "the firm with critical resources (contributions) and in exchange each expects its interests to be satisfied (by inducements)"
Brenner (1993: 205)	"having some legitimate, non-trivial relationship with an organization (such as) exchange transactions, action impacts, and moral responsibilities"

(continued)

Table 1.1 (continued)

Source	Stake
Carroll (1993: 60)	"asserts to have one or more of these kinds of stakes in the business" – may be affected or affect …
Freeman (1994: 415)	participants in "the human process of value creation"
Wicks et al. (1994: 483)	"interact with and give meaning and definition to the corporation"
Langtry (1994: 433)	"the firm is significantly responsible for their well-being, or they hold a moral or legal claim on the firm"
Starik (1994: 90)	"can or are making their stakes known" – "are or might be influenced by, or are or potentially are influencers or some organization"
Clarkson (1995: 5)	"bear some form of risk as a result of having invested some form of capital, human or financial, something of value, in a firm" or "are placed at risk as a result of a firm's activities"
Clarkson (1995: 106)	"have, or claim, ownership, rights, or interests in a corporation and its activities"
Näsi (1995: 19)	"interact with the firm and thus make its operation possible"
Brenner (1995: 76, Note 1)	"do or which could impact or be impacted by the firm/organization"
Donaldson and Preston (1995: 85)	"persons or groups with legitimate interests in procedural and/or substantive aspects of corporate activity"

Source: Mitchell et al. (1997: 858–859)

These contradictory elements provided the point of departure for an intense debate in which the term "stakeholder" was transformed from a play on words into a notion and, finally, into a strategic management problematic which has, since 1984, generated a substantial amount of academic output. Between the year in which *Strategic Management: A Stakeholder Approach* was published, and 2010, which saw the appearance of *Stakeholder Theory: The State of the Art*, *Strategic Management*, and *Stakeholders*, a plurality of hypotheses and controversies were developed, illustrating how attractive the theory is. At any event, the notion of the "stakeholder" makes it possible to develop a theory which offers a representation of power within a structure of governance, namely that of the corporation, thereby shining an analytical light on corporate governance and the strategic decision-making processes of the firm.

Conceptual Framework: R. E. Freeman (1984–2010) and His Followers

Freeman, a philosopher and Professor of Strategic Management, has always recognized the diversity of his intellectual heritage, which ranges from Ackoff to the logical and pragmatic philosophers. Indeed, a certain number of mostly American researchers and consultants have followed in his footsteps, including Agle, Boatright, Bowie, Clarkson, Donaldson, Dunfee, French, Goodpaster, Harrison, Jones, Kochan, Marens, Mitchell, Parmer, Phillips, Venkataraman, Wicks and Wood.

But the role of the firm and the nature of its obligations to the rest of society had been analyzed and discussed long before Freeman. After the 1929 crisis, Dodd (1932) and Barnard (1938) advanced the idea that the corporation should balance the rival interests of its various participants with a view to ensuring their continued cooperation. After the 1929 crash, a number of major companies, including General Electric, recognized four actors as stakeholders: customers, employees, the community and stockholders (Hummels 1998). Other authors examined the question of the identity of the main groups participating in the identity of the firm. Rhenman and Stymne (1965, quoted by Carroll and Näsi 1997) describe the firm as a social and technical system in which stakeholders play a decisive role; they are, for example, at the origin of experiments in industrial democracy in Scandinavia. Blair (1995) posits that the symbolic foundations of the theory are to be found in the case brought against Ford by the Dodge brothers in 1919, when the Michigan Supreme Court found in favor of stockholders who had demanded that the company should share its profits in the form of dividends. But surely this episode has only limited relevance to a theory which makes a clear distinction between stakeholders and stockholders.

Robert Edward Freeman

Robert Edward Freeman was born on December 18, 1951 in Columbus, Georgia, USA. After studying Philosophy and Mathematics at Duke University in the 1970s, he gained a PhD in Philosophy at Washington University in St. Louis in 1978. In the early 1980s, he worked as a researcher in the Wharton Business School's Busch Center, directed by Russell Lincoln Ackoff, a pioneer in operational research and systems theory. He then moved to the Wharton Applied Research Center, recently set up by Ackoff (an academic), and James R. Emshoff (a businessman). These last set up and supported a research seminar on the notion of the "stakeholder." The mission of the center was to act as "Wharton's window on the world," but after the initial seminar, the participants asked themselves whether the subject was not too normative, revealing as it did questions about distributive justice which no one present could answer. It was then that the fortune of stakeholder theory was indissociably linked to R. E. Freeman's career trajectory.

Freeman, a philosopher, worked simultaneously with experts in strategy and sociologists. The idea of stakeholder theory was congruent with the ideas expressed by Ackoff in his 1974 book, *Redesigning the Future*, written with Ian Mitroff and Richard Mason. Furthermore, Wharton was in contact with the Stanford Research Institute where Igor Ansoff, Eric Rhenman, Robert

(continued)

(continued)

Stewart and Marion Doscher were developing strategic planning and strategic assumptions analysis. Emshoff, President of Indecap, encouraged Freeman to start writing about stakeholder management. That was how he came into contact with AT & T and Bell and, in conjunction with the center, produced an evaluation of the strategy applied by a Mexican brewery. Simultaneously, Freeman collaborated regularly with Bill Evan, a sociologist from the University of Pennsylvania. Evan immediately saw in the notion of the stakeholder the possibility of democratizing large companies. He regarded it as a concrete idea that could be applied in real life. The objectives of the Wharton seminar and those of the sociologist coincided. Thanks to Bill Evan, Freeman learned to reconcile philosophy, the social sciences and management and, as he later wrote, "continue to be the philosopher that he was, rather than a positivist social scientist." In 1984, he published *Strategic Management: A Stakeholder Approach*. In 1993, he co-wrote an article with Evan on Kantian capitalism. Simultaneously, Freeman was appointed as Professor of Management at the public sector University of Minnesota, an establishment with over 50,000 students. In 1986, his appointment to the highly prestigious Darden School of the University of Virginia, itself founded by Thomas Jefferson, saw him return to the southeast United States. In the same year, the Olsson Center, focusing on Applied Ethics was set up, and, in 2004, Freeman became head of the Business Roundtable Institute where he taught business ethics to middle-managers in large companies. In Virginia, a conservative state, at once the home of American Republicanism and characterized by deep-seated religious and ethical values, Freeman focused on business ethics and corporate governance. It was thus that, in his wake, in 1999, A. C. Wicks, head of the Olsson Center, produced a convergent theory of stakeholder theory, which he has been developing ever since; J.S Harrison, Professor of Strategy at the Robins School at the University of Richmond (Virginia) defends Freeman's vision in the Academy of Management, an association of which most academics working in the field of management are members. In 2010, the three authors published a *State of the Art* of stakeholder theory. R. A. Philips, also a professor of the Robins School, is one of the most productive researchers in the field. In 2010, conjointly with Freeman, he published a book simply entitled, *Stakeholders*.

Russell L. Ackoff (1974, 1994) seems to have been the first to have genuinely recognized the conceptual potential of the notion of stakeholders. He oriented his research toward a representation of the corporation and developed an embryonic form of stakeholder theory by defining the objectives of organizations. According to Ackoof, the corporation should reconcile the contradictory interests of groups to which it is directly linked, adjusting its objectives with a view to satisfying the needs of those groups in an equitable manner. Although profit is one of its objectives, it is not the only one. But, with the exception of Ackoff and a number of authors working between the late 1960s and the mid-1980s, the theory received little attention in the fields of management, strategy and ethics. Indeed, when Freeman presented an article on stakeholder for publication, the evaluators suggested that he should perhaps use the term "stockholder" instead.

The most all-encompassing version of stakeholder theory is the one outlined in 1984 (republished in 2010) by Freeman in *Strategic Management: A Stakeholder Approach*. In his book, Freeman suggests that the generally separate concepts of the organization and the corporation should be linked to produce a strategic, political and moral conception which includes negotiation and communication. For the author, the corporation is a wheel whose spokes represent particular interests (Aggeri 2008; Cazal 2011). This observation is based on the dependence of firms on third parties, these last expressing requests concerned with risks engendered by economic activity. It is in this context that Freeman's key concept (1984) acquires its full meaning: "Simply put, a stakeholder is any group or individual who can affect, or is affected by, the achievement of the organization's objectives." According to the American professor, stakeholders include any group or individual who can either help or analyze a corporation by calling its strategy into question. By focusing on these groups and their wellbeing, whether they are internal or external to the corporation, it should be possible for an organization to establish its strategies by ensuring that they are consonant with societal expectations. Nevertheless, this approach requires a theoretical framework in order to deal with various groups, which are not merely aggregations of particular interests. Thus, theoretical research into the role of stakeholders would provide a concrete analytical context making it possible to examine in a relevant way the relationship between the corporation and its internal and external environment. With this in mind, Freeman starts by drawing up a map of the stakeholders in a specific firm. He then analyzes potential negotiation processes based on specific themes concerning particular groups of stakeholders. Negotiation is, in this context, based on dialogue, with a view to guaranteeing free and voluntary collaboration (Freeman 1984: 74). Later, Freeman (1984: 83) demonstrated that stakeholder theory could be used to define the fundamental visions and aims of a corporation. Analyzing stakeholders is the same thing as analyzing the values and social problems by which the corporation is confronted. From the author's point of view, this analysis is a part of the value of the corporation, enabling it to measure not just its financial value but also its social and societal performance (Fig. 1.1).

With *Strategic Management: A Stakeholder Approach* (1984), Freeman became a pioneer who, not content with underlining the need for a theoretical framework (the creation of value by stakeholders versus the creation of financial value) suggested new approaches to elaborating corporate strategy. His approach to the objectives of the corporation and to how it fitted into its environment overturned the traditional frameworks of strategy. Responding to directors and shareholders who remained unconvinced of the relevance of his representation of the firm, he maintained that, in respecting stakeholders, the firm would be better able to make profits.

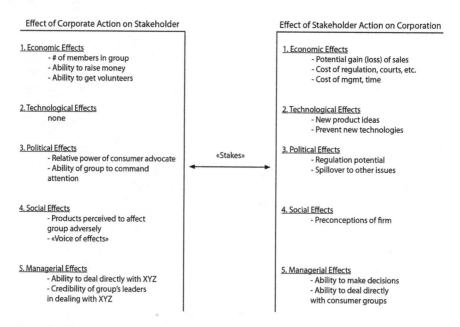

Fig. 1.1 Impact of the corporation on stakeholders/Impact of stakeholders on the corporation (Source: R.E. Freeman, Strategic Management, Pitman Publishing Inc, Boston, 1984)

In sum, *Strategic Management: A Stakeholder Approach* suggests a pragmatic approach. Indeed, Freeman has always claimed to belong to a pragmatic current (Freeman et al. 2010). In this instance, pragmatism means that identifying and negotiating with stakeholders is the best way of advancing and developing business. Consequently, as Freeman has explained on a number of occasions, stakeholder theory is an operational theory enabling firms not only to define and develop their strategy, but also to evaluate it.

Parameters of the Theory

After 30 years of controversy, we can now say that stakeholder theory is principally a theory of corporate strategy which has been taken up by researchers in the fields of business ethics, organization theory, political and moral philosophy (Phillips et al. 2003), political sociology and political science. In many strategic management encyclopedias, such as those published in 2001 and 2005, stakeholder theory is presented as a promising and idiosyncratic approach.

In effect, stakeholder theory is a recent and increasingly important current in the field of strategy (Freeman 1984, 2001; Martinet 1984; Martinet and Reynaud 2001). The current is concerned with reappraising the concept of the corporation, dominated by agency theory (Jensen and Meckling 1976; Jensen 2000), which considers the organization exclusively in terms of its ability to create value for shareholders. Noble Prize-winner Milton Friedman declared in the *New York Times* in 1970 that "the social responsibility of business is to increase its profits." Since profits are the result of an implicit contract with non-shareholders, each group of non-shareholders has a contractual relationship with the corporation in that they all receive payment (employees) that they freely accept. The financial objective not only serves the interests of the owners of the corporation but also provides a framework which makes it possible to ensure that limited resources are allocated, managed and deployed as effectively as possible (Stewart 1994). But this approach describes the corporation as a combination of production factors which transform "inputs" into "outputs," which, in turn, create value by being sold on competitive markets (Martinet 1984). In stakeholder theory, the corporation is not exclusively based on the particular interests of its owners and stakeholders. *Shareholder value* (short term) can thus be contrasted to *stakeholder value* (medium- to long-term). That is why the choice of value creation through stakeholders is, above all, strategic (medium-term, long-term), informed as it is by the twin objectives of survival and development. But by making that choice, the corporation is confronted with agents (other than shareholders) which limit its access to resources. The presence of these agents obliges it to develop a competitive strategy which satisfies a range of interests. The corporation thus attempts to build within a society and not merely in a market (Martinet 1984).

The strategic management of stakeholders is primarily based on a capacity to understand their expectations as a factor in the development of the organization, and to acknowledge their contribution to value creation, be they internal (investors, the ensemble of collaborators) or external (consumers, suppliers, civil society, public authorities) to the corporation. With this aim in mind, the corporation is encouraged to define the nature of its relationship with its stakeholders (Thomson et al. 1991). These interests are *de facto* "stakeholders" in the strategic policies of the corporation (Freeman 1981, 1984, 2007, 2010; Hitt et al. 2001). The corporation thus "manages" on behalf of its stakeholders (Freeman 2007). But what does managing on behalf of one's stakeholders imply?

Attempts to separate the economic from the social represent a stumbling block which continuously threatens corporate legitimacy. While capitalism guarantees the corporation a degree of autonomy based on an *a priori* trust in economic actors – specifically, in private firms (which oil the wheels of the economy), that autonomy is also based on an *a priori* trust in society, since the corporation's institutional legitimacy underpins its right to make profits freely without the need for self-justification. However, the fact that its pragmatic legitimacy is often contested encourages the corporation to recognize its dependence on external factors. It is here that the idea of corporate social responsibility emerges. Stakeholder theory is part of a debate about the role of business in society. Like business ethics, it highlights the way in which the economic sphere is socially embedded. In effect, if one takes the view that the corporation exists not only in the market, but also in society, then the sociality of the

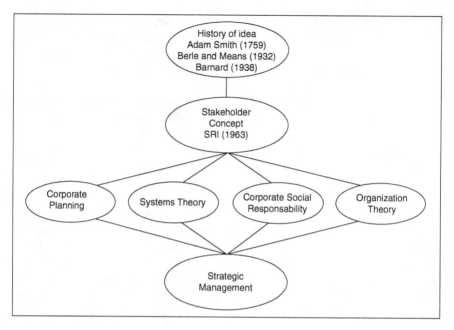

Fig. 1.2   A history of the stakeholder concept

economy and the embeddedness of the corporation in society is a given. This observation originates in Karl Polanyi's *The Great Transformation* (1944). The advent of
globalization has led to an increasing recognition of the embedded nature of the
corporation. But a variety of approaches are taken to the phenomenon. More than a
moralizing approach external to economic activity, stakeholder theory deals prag-
matically and strategically with the issue. That is why business ethics encompasses,
in the shape of stakeholder theory, a strategic aspect (Fig. 1.2).

Epistemological Debates and Theoretical Pluralism

While in the 1980s only one article on stakeholder theory was published in a leading
management journal, from the 1990s an increasing number of articles and books on
the subject began to appear. Between 2000 and 2007, 135 articles were published in
the eight leading international management and business ethics journals (Laplume
et al. 2008). This trend gave rise to a form of theoretical, methodological and practical pluralism.

Is Stakeholder Theory a Theory?

Is stakeholder theory a *bona fide* theory? In English, the term "stakeholder view" is generally preferred. For Freeman, it is more of a "genre" than a theory (Hitt et al. 2001). But could it not be seen as a as a kind of practical methodology based on a more general theory, that of a civil society backed up by the economic and geostrategic power of the multinationals (Bonnafous-Boucher and Porcher 2010). If so, the corporation would have to guarantee the rule of law in the same way that the state does in the classical, Hegelian theory of civil society (Bonnafous-Boucher 2006; Bonnafous-Boucher and Porcher 2010). However, as far as we are aware, it is not the role of the corporation to guarantee the rule of law, even if certain political scientists and legal experts attempt to replace civil society with a society made up of stakeholders (Ackerman and Alstot 1999). It is thus legitimate to question the unifying ambitions of a theory which is applicable to numerous fields, including business ethics, strategy, law, economics and organization theory (Freeman and Philips 2002: 333).

A Concrete Theory: Categorizing the Actors Who Count in Corporate Strategy

The effectiveness of a unifying theory is conditioned by two issues, both of which have been addressed by researchers, namely, the identity of stakeholders, and who really counts and for whom (Mitchell et al. 1997).

Identifying the Stakeholders First, it is evident that stakeholders are not necessarily individuals. They can be a group, an organization, an institution, an association, or a thing, for example an aspect of the natural environment. But if this is true, then surely anything could be a stakeholder. Unsurprisingly, authors have asked who is a stakeholder and who isn't. The confusion caused by an exaggeratedly broad conception of the notion prompted Bowie (1988a, b), Freeman (1994) and Näsi (1995) to attempt to formulate a more specific definition. An essential criterion was introduced: stakeholders were invoked when the survival of an organization or a corporation was dependent on one or more third parties. Although this definition is not often applied (stakeholders are generally thought of as groups or individuals influenced by and influencing the organization), it does nevertheless represent progress in terms of the recognition of stakeholders. The task of strategic management is thus to identify the third parties concerned and to decide how to work with those parties. This approach means that the strategic context is no longer exclusively associated with gaining a competitive edge (Porter 1985). The corporation once again becomes the center from which expectations, stakes and interests, be they convergent or divergent, are analyzed (Table 1.2).

Table 1.2 Specific expectations of different stakeholders

Partenaires	Les attentes directes des *Stakeholders*	Informations fournies par les entreprises
Salariés	Rémunération, sécurité de l'emploi, formation	Rapports de l'entreprise, nouvelles sur l'entreprise, négociations
Actionnaires	Dividendes et appréciation du cours boursier	Rapports et comptes annuels, informations sur les fusions et les OPA
Clients	Qualité, service, sécurité, bon rapport qualité-prix	Publicité, documentations, entretien
Banquiers	Liquidité et solvabilité de l'entreprise, valeur des garanties, production de trésorerie	Ratios de couverture, nantissement, prévision de trésorerie
Fournisseurs	Ratation stable et durable	Paiement dans les délais
Gouvernement	Respect des lois, de l'emploi, de la compétitivité et données fidéles	Rapports aux organisms officiels, communiqués de presse
Public	Sécurité des opérations, contribution à la communauté	Rapports sur la sécurité, reportages
Environment	Substitution des ressources non durables et activités non polluantes	Rapports sur l' environnement. Rapports de conformité

Source: Clarke T, "The Stakeholder Corporation: A Business Philosophy for the Information Age", *Long Range Planning*, 1998, 31/2,182–194. The table was taken and adapted from Caby (2003)

Translation

Partners	Direct stakeholder expectations	Information supplied by firms
Employees	Remuneration, job security, training	Company reports, news about the firm, negotiations
Shareholders	Dividends and increase in share value	Annual reports and accounts, information about mergers and acquisitions
Clients	Quality, service, security, value for money	Publicity, documentation, maintenance
Bankers	Liquidity and solvency of the firm, value of guarantees cash flow	Coverage ratios, collateral, cash flow forecasts
Suppliers	Stable long-term rotation	Prompt payment
Government	Respect for the law, employment, competitiveness, accurate data	Reports for official bodies, press releases
Public	Operational safety, contribution to community	Safety reports, reportages
Environment	Replacement of non-sustainable resources, non-polluting activities	Environmental reports, compliance reports

In the wake of these various clarifications, classifications designed to identify stakeholders have given rise to an abundant literature. Aware of the difficulty of identifying all the stakeholders in an organization, some authors have attempted to establish categories of actors. These authors have focused on the task of generalizing categories of actors beyond cases of specific firms.

The Hierarchy and Typology of Mitchell, Agle and Wood One of the most effective stakeholder classifications is that of Mitchell et al. (1997). Their classification is based on three questions: What real or potential power do stakeholders have in society enabling them to impose their will on a corporation? What kind of legitimacy do they possess? And how urgently does an organization have to respond to their demands? When the interests of stakeholders do not converge with those of either the corporation or other stakeholders, the parties are obliged to negotiate. Negotiation can be approached in different ways depending on the perceptions of various stakeholders and the way in which they themselves are perceived. Groups possessing the three qualities (power, legitimacy, urgency) are termed *definitive stakeholders* and are thus included in the negotiation process. The degree of participation of various actors depends on the number of qualities they possess. Those with two attributes – urgency and legitimacy – are considered *dependent stakeholders*. But stakeholders with power and urgency can be dangerous. Stakeholders with power and legitimacy are termed *dominant*. Those with only one attribute are termed *dormant* (power), *discretionary* (legitimacy), or *demanding* (urgency) (Fig. 1.3).

There are other, less operational and less relevant classifications than Mitchell et al.'s (1997). These classifications are based on an initial distinction between primary and secondary stakeholders. Some of them are content to distinguish between internal and external stakeholders. While this distinction is a practical one, it is also simplistic in that it does not take the relational content of the theory into account. It also fails to take account of the ubiquity of stakeholders (Martinet 1984) in the

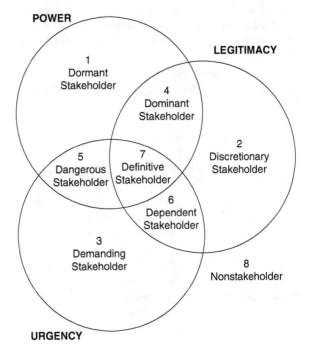

Fig. 1.3 Stakeholder typology (Mitchell, Agle and Wood) (Source: Mitchell, Agle and Wood, "Toward a Theory of Stakeholder Identification and Salience: Defining the Principle of Who and What Really Counts", *The Academy of Management Review*, 1997, 22/4, 874)

POWER

LEGITIMACY

1
Dormant
Stakeholder

4
Dominant
Stakeholder

2
Discretionary
Stakeholder

5
Dangerous
Stakeholder

7
Definitive
Stakeholder

6
Dependent
Stakeholder

3
Demanding
Stakeholder

8
Nonstakeholder

URGENCY

shape of actors within the corporation and outside it. In effect, an employee can also be a consumer of the products he or she manufactures. Thus, the relationship between the stakeholders and the corporation takes on a particular importance for Cornell and Shapiro (1987), Freeman and Evan (1990), and Hill and Jones (1992). All of these authors talk of contracting parties. It could also be added that the analysis of the relationship between stakeholders (and not only between the corporation and its stakeholders) establishes a non-dual explanatory framework which does not refer the corporation back to a faceoff with all that is external to it. Thus, in its diagnostic and management approaches, the corporation has to deal with unusual alliances or with the divergent interests of individual stakeholders.

Two years before Mitchell, Agle and Wood published their typology, Clarkson (1995) distinguished between stakeholders who take on risk by investing human or financial capital, and those who do not take any risk. For the author, stakeholders fall into two categories: voluntary and involuntary. In this sense, a stakeholder is someone who has everything to lose and who will thus make legitimate claims based on the risks he or she has run. In this case, shareholders are clearly considered *stakeholders*, as are entrepreneurs. Indeed, why not? But surely this veers away from the stakeholder approach which, from the outset, has made a distinction between *stakeholders* and *shareholders* and presented an alternative to the orthodox vision of corporate governance.

Other, secondary, typologies focus on different categories of actors: *public actors* (Tichy et al. 1997); *archetypal actors* (shareholders, employees, clients, suppliers); *recognized actors* (banks, insurance companies, enterprise networks, unions, public authorities, international organizations, civic associations, NGOs); *controversial actors* (competitors, the media, activists, the natural environment) (Lépineux 2005). Mention could also be made of *tertiary* stakeholders, those which do not have the capacity to speak for themselves, for example natural elements (oceans, mountains, animals), and future generations (Starik 1994). Some authors have also talked of *silent* or *mute* stakeholders represented by third parties (NGOs) who plead on their behalf.

Typologies and classifications, particularly that of Mitchell et al., are useful in that they furnish an actionable model which can be used to make decisions and negotiate for and with stakeholders. But, let's not be naive, they can also be used against them. The theory can always be instrumentalized. Regardless of their degree of sophistication, the limit of such typologies is to be found in the way in which they represent society as a series of actors of varying value (or threat) to the corporation (and particularly to the very large corporation). One of the key factors in Agle et al.'s typology is the hierarchization of categories of actors in function of the interests of the firm. In this sense, although stakeholder theory makes it possible to represent the actors, the typologies developed do not focus on the interests and issues that they bring to the fore. From this point of view, stakeholder theory can be criticized on the grounds that it offers only a partial conception of civil society, which it considers as a series of self-centered, interest-based struggles. In our opinion, an analysis of the controversies and arguments on which the motivations of stakeholders are based would make it possible to take into account issues originating beyond specific groups of actors. In terms of typologies, it should also be noted that exhaustive investigations of lists of actors are of only limited value, even if probability calculus is used.

A Theoretical Pluralism Revealed by Donaldson and Preston (1995)

The perspective from which issues are identified, and from which the relationship between stakeholders and the organization is dealt with, exerts an influence on theoretical perspectives elaborated by researchers. Three approaches to the theory have been identified.

The descriptive approach to stakeholders reveals a constellation of cooperative and competing interests (Moore 1999). It describes the growing complexity of organizations (multinationals, transnational companies, subcontracting networks and associations). It explains the conditions of emergence of new forms of organization that encompass multiple interests (Kochan and Rubinstein 2000). It takes account of relationships between the organization and the environment by calling into question the environment as an objective given, or, in other words, as an ensemble of forces external to the organization and beyond its control (Desreumaux and Selznick 2009). And it helps to articulate various organizational levels – intra, inter, external – by mitigating the dichotomy between the organization's internal environment (components), and its external environment (degree of complexity, stability, availability of resources).

The advantage of the descriptive approach is that, despite its explicative nature, it can also be applied instrumentally as a methodological framework (Caroll and Bucholtz 2000). It provides strategic analysis since, while dealing with the task of identifying stakeholders, it also attempts to manage them. In this sense, the theory is a decision-making tool for directors.

The instrumental approach is close to the strategic vision of the corporation: it aims to manage the firm vis-à-vis the stakeholders with a view to reconciling its profit and performance with other interests which influence it either directly or indirectly. It not only identifies stakeholders but also measures their relative influence (Jones and Wicks 1999; Hosseini and Brenner 1992), comparing the triple bottom line and the interests of the corporation by postulating that the more it satisfies expectations, the more it grows. However, the shortcoming of this approach is that it telescopes divergent interests into a knot of contracts between shareholders, directors and stakeholders. The arena of negotiation is triangular, open only to the interests of the three parties. Nevertheless, advocates of certain currents of the instrumentalist approach attempt to reconcile this paradoxical aspect of the theory (Goodpaster 1991) by claiming that the idea according to which shareholders and stakeholders have specific obligations is contradictory. The concept of the "balanced scorecard" means that the corporation must take into account three areas of

performance: environmental, social and economic. Another instrumental application is based on the profit a corporation can pass on to its stakeholders. This approach
was described by Jones (1995). However, it is legitimate to ask if an operational
conception of the theory is necessarily associated with an instrumental approach.

The normative approach insists on the intrinsic legitimacy of the expectations of
stakeholders even when the response to those expectations is not closely linked to
the survival of the corporation. The normative approach becomes an ethical theory
when it enjoins the corporation to act responsibly vis-à-vis its stakeholders (corporate stakeholder responsibility). Several professional codes, values and corporate
missions are inspired by the concept of stakeholders, for example those promoted
by the Caux Roundtable (1994). Clarkson (1998) develops responsible management
principles based on the notion of the stakeholder. According to these principles,
managers must be aware of the legitimacy of interests external to the firm because
its activities represent a risk to society. Since stakeholders are vulnerable, managers
must be aware of any conflicts that they might engender. This conception gives ethics a strategic dimension.

In affirming the intrinsic legitimacy of stakeholders (Donaldson and Preston
1995), the normative approach provides them with access to corporate governance,
thus once more linking business ethics to strategy (Gibson 2000). But we are touching here on the limits of the normative approach in that governance is exercised
within the framework of asset-based salaried capitalism. "Asset-based" because
shareholders traditionally invest capital in order to increase their assets. "Asset-
based and salaried" because the capital invested does not only come from professional investors but also from private individuals, for example pension funds created
by commercial banking products (life insurance, retirement savings plans), and
human capital in the form of the corporation's human resources. While stakeholder
theory is associated with a break with the traditional (and often simplified) representation of shareholder value (Charreaux and Wirtz 2006), it nevertheless adheres
to a contemporary framework of governance, that of an asset-based salaried capitalism, presupposing open participation on the part of stakeholders. The presupposi-
tion is that all stakeholders can become shareholders. The theory aims to broaden
the scope of asset-based capitalism. What, then, is the future of the normative
approach? The formation of a collective interest in the activities of the corporation
expressing itself in the form of a recognized objective accepted by the stakeholders?
(Aglietta and Rebérioux 2004).

The three approaches suggested by Donaldson and Preston provide a reassuring
framework for those willing to immerge themselves in an abundant, often iterative,
and sometimes confusing literature. Unifying its various aspects, Wicks (1999) provides a convergent theory of the stakeholder approach. But the question remains –
are the three approaches (descriptive, instrumental and normative) irreconcilable or
can a synthesis be achieved? In the same year, Freeman addressed the entire academic management science community, asserting that there was no neutral form of
stakeholder theory and calling for divergent approaches (Freeman 1999).

Critiques of the Theory

In 2010, at the start of his book on the state of the art of stakeholder theory (Freeman 2010: 3), the author identifies his adversaries as Milton Friedman, Michael Jensen, Michael Porter, and Oliver Williamson. Let us examine the main critiques levied at Freeman.

First, stakeholder theory is criticized on the methodological level: without identifying stakeholders precisely and defining their role in corporate governance, everything and everyone is a stakeholder and the frontiers of the theory are so porous that any number of interpretations are possible, thus depriving the theory of all credibility. *Second*, the normative and ethical approach to the theory (Phillips et al. 2003) has been called into question by the advocates of an orthodox style of governance – a focus on stakeholders enables managers pursuing their own personal interests to make subjective choices. According to this perspective, the theory offers an excuse for managers not to promote the interests of the corporation's shareholders and owners. If the expectations of stakeholders are taken into account, the corporation no longer has a single objective (profit) and it becomes impossible to manage by applying an approach based on economic rationality (Jensen 2000: 236). (To this it can be objected that, in spite of its complexity, stakeholder theory serves the cause of the maximization of corporate profit). Third, from an opposing viewpoint, the theory often provides a fragmentary vision of the relationship between stakeholders and the organization. The relationship is generally seen from a single perspective whether in terms of the relationship of the corporation vis-à-vis its stakeholders (instrumental approach) or of the stakeholders vis-à-vis the corporation (normative approach). Relationships between the stakeholders themselves are rarely envisaged. However, the social and democratic conception which attempts to render social justice possible in a capitalist system of production in a social democracy makes it possible to take into account the inter-relationship between a plurality of stakes and interests by relativizing the dualism of interests between the corporation, on the one hand, and stakeholders, on the other. *Fourth and last*, stakeholder theory calls into question the meaning of a regional ethics, such as business ethics. In effect, in our view the theory possesses a universal value even if it is associated with a particular ethical perspective (business ethics) (Table 1.3).

By comparing a number of critiques, we have obtained a clearer image of stakeholder theory, which displays a certain degree of porosity in regard to fields which are generally kept separate: the market and politics; philosophical theories of action, on the one hand, and theories of management, on the other; various fields of knowledge. Stakeholder theory's conception of management thus implies a recognition not only of the corporation's place in the economic market but also of the social structure of society.

Table 1.3 The limits of stakeholder theory. What the theory isn't

Critical distortions	Friendly misinterpretations
Stakeholder theory is an excuse for managerial opportunism (Jensen 2001; Marcoux 2000; Sternberg 2000)	Stakeholder theory requires changes to current law (Hendry 2001a, b; Van Buren 2001)
Stakeholder theory cannot provide a sufficiently specific objective function for the corporation (Jensen 2001)	Stakeholder theory is socialism and refers to the entire economy (Barnett 1997; Hutton 1995; Rustin 1997)
Stakeholder theory is primarily concerned with distribution of financial outputs (Marcoux 2000)	Stakeholder theory is a comprehensive moral doctrine (Orts and Studler 2002)
Allstakeholders must be treated equally (Gioia 1999; Marcoux 2000; Sternberg 2000)	Stakeholder theory applies only to corporations (Donaldson and Preston 1995)

Source: *Stakeholder Theory and Organizational Ethics*, Robert Phillips, Berrett-Koahler Publishers, San Francisco, 2003

The Scope of the Theory and Its Potential for Expansion

Stakeholder theory is at its apogee and the range of interpretations to which it has been subject means that it possesses significant heuristic capacity and potential for expansion. However, these qualities were not noticed immediately and the theory is still almost exclusively viewed as an alternative to the orthodox financial approach (agency theory) to corporate governance. Inscribed from the outset in the fields of administrative and management science (disciplines long depreciated by other disciplines on the grounds that they are too performative), its scope, or one would have imagined, could only have been local. But while the theory was developing, the role of the corporation at the center of the public space was posing questions that called for answers. Far from being marginal, the theory, with its multiplicity of variants and currents, is fecund in a number of different ways; indeed, over the course of the years, it has imposed itself as an explanatory vector of contemporary currents of liberalism and capitalism.

From the point of view of stakeholders (whether those influenced by the activities of organizations or the "damned of the earth"), the theory touches upon political philosophy, political sociology and studies in international relations by pointing civil society toward a civil society of international stakeholders in which negotiation becomes a flexible regulatory framework. Consequently, it is based on a potentially voluntary agreement between stakeholders with divergent interests (social contract theories). Moreover, it reappraises the nature of theories of distributive justice popular in certain currents of liberalism (Rawls, *Theory of Justice*). Still from the point of view of political philosophy, Philips, following Rawls, appeals to the idea of fairness, and develops the possibility of achieving a greater degree of equity and justice by accommodating stakeholders within the management process. "Organizational justice" (Philips 2003b) implies that the interests of all members of the organization, as well as all those outside it should be respected. The concept of fairness becomes an essential component of stakeholder theory. From the point of view of moral philosophy, it partakes of the traditional theory of the common good. Although the common good is a common denominator that individuals living in society seek out and define for themselves, it cannot be viewed purely and simply as an aggregation of the needs and interests of individuals. It is a political, moral and practical quest for the smallest and largest common denominator enabling us to live together (sovereign good). Dialoguing with stakeholders would be the best gauge of access to a definition of the common good. By extension, the quest for the common good is associated with an approach to political and moral philosophy based on Aristotelian propositions (*Nicomachean Ethics*). Although, in the social sciences, stakeholder theory poses an open question to the sociology of actors (Crozier and Friedberg 1977), it is closer to Actor-Network Theory or ANT (Latour 1984; Callon 1986; Akrich 1987). In effect, the essential problem addressed by stakeholder theory is not related to the identification of groups, but, rather, to the concept of "relationships" and actor networks (for example, the relationship between the organization, powerful stakeholders and dormant stakeholders). As such, stakeholder theory questions the systemic conceptions of organization theory. As in the systemic approach to engineering, biology and sociology of the post-war period (Wiewer 1948; Bertalanffy 1968; Crozier and Friedberg 1977), it represents the organization as a coherent ensemble in dynamic interaction with its environment. But what creates a system is the combination and association of mediations which hold it together by translating arguments and enabling actors (individuals and groups) to define themselves.

In the final analysis, the theory serves as a bridge between contemporary political and moral philosophy, economic policy and management.

From the point of view of the corporation, stakeholder theory provides an alternative conception of corporate governance; it accords business ethics a strategic role; it offers a new, systemic theory of organization which accords a place to ecological concerns; it contributes to research in the field of marketing (Knox and Gruar 2007); and it can be applied to developing a strategic vision of human resources in which the corporation as a social body is reflected in all its diversity, with all its roles receiving due consideration. Last, far from being an abstract theory, it seeks to be actionable. Freeman is a philosopher and researcher who bases his analytical method on pragmatism. He has given his theory a universalist aspect (Evan and Freeman 1993). He supposes that the theory defends the universal rights of stakeholders.

Could the theory be exported to disciplines in which it has not yet found its place, such as the study of public policy? Although the term "stakeholder" is much used by both theorists and practitioners of political life, they are not necessarily referring to the theory, whose central focus is on the relationship between the corporation and its environment. Care should be taken in regard to the extension of the theory, for such an extension would risk encompassing not only the relationship between the corporation and its stakeholders, but also the whole of society conceived of as stakeholders. This may lead to society being represented, in the

American manner, as being composed of pressure groups and interest groups (Courty 2006). But as Phillips and Freeman observe (Freeman and Phillips 2002), there is a difference of principle between the organizational level and the social level. The view taken here, however, is that the most promising interpretation of stakeholder theory is as a political and moral philosophy providing democratic foundations and principles relevant to all forms of governance.

Chapter 2
Stakeholder Theory in Strategic Management

Strategy consists in making choices and taking decisions involving an organization while being aware of the interactions between the corporation, its environment, and its existing or potential resources. Linked to corporate policy, it is an activity which requires reflection and action. As *practice*, it "gradually constructs ensembles of opportunities and imagines trajectories of development in a rapidly changing and partially unpredictable environment" (Desreumaux et al. 2005, 2006). As *reflection*, it "renders the world comprehensible, simplifying it with a view to facilitating action" (Desreumaux et al. 2005, 2006). As such, it is *praxeological reflection* because it seeks efficacy and efficiency (yields and the relationship between assets and results) (Martinet et al. 1990). From the outset, stakeholder theory has cast itself as a practical and useful theory associated with strategy, as is demonstrated by both the oldest and most recent publications on the subject, those of Freeman and his co-authors: *Stakeholder Theory*, written by Phillipps and Freeman (2010); *Stakeholder Theory: A State of the Art*, coordinated by Freeman et al. (2010); *The Handbook of Strategic Management*, edited by Hitt et al. (2001); *Strategic Management: A Stakeholder Approach* (1984); "Manager les parties prenantes" (1982); and *Manager pour les parties prenantes: survie, réputation et succès* (2007). To this list can be added the recent book by Wicks, Freeman and Werhane: *Business Ethics: A Managerial Approach* (2009). For the advocates of the theory, the managerial or strategic management approach encompasses planning, systems theory, corporate social responsibility, and organization theory.

But in spite of its origins and embeddedness in strategy, stakeholder theory has long been contested as an operational model for corporations. Yet, over the course of the last decade, many companies (from those listed on the CAC40 to mid-sized firms and small family enterprises (Bingham et al. 2010) have drawn up stakeholder maps, identifying stakeholders in order to negotiate with them in function of strategic priorities. These maps are an acknowledgement of the theory's usefulness. But other advantages should be highlighted: (1) Stakeholder theory reconciles strategy and ethics to provide an approach to analyzing the purposes of economic action rather than merely attempting to moralize the actions of business leaders. (2)

© The Author(s) 2016
M. Bonnafous-Boucher, J.D. Rendtorff, *Stakeholder Theory*, SpringerBriefs in Ethics, DOI 10.1007/978-3-319-44356-0_2

It offers a representation of the "management of management" (Perez 2003) and of governance as a space of negotiation and deliberation about value creation. In other words, it defines corporate governance as something more than just the rules pertaining in boards of directors, and this when most of the finance literature (Shleifer and Vishny 1997) restricts it to the dominant definition of governance [which] covers all the mechanisms that guarantee various lenders a return on investment, while preventing directors and dominant shareholders from appropriating excessive value (Wirtz 2008). (3). It focuses on a conception of economic activity and strategy that depends on (because it is related to) its environment. Before being a group or individual that influences or is influenced by the corporation, stakeholders are "symbiotes," or, in other words, "those elements of the environment on which the corporation is dependent for inputs" (Freeman 2010, 86, quoting MacMillan 1978: 66). The term "symbiote" means that each element pursues a sort of symbiosis with the environment. (4). This aspect of the theory is a rich source of information for management science and entrepreneurship, this last field promoting above all the heroic action of free and voluntarist creators whose actions are not dependent on any social, legal or cultural context. This did not escape Venkataraman (2002: 46) for whom, "the essence of the corporation is the competitive claims made on it by diverse stakeholders. It is a fact of business life that different stakeholders have different and often conflicting expectations of a corporation."

Consequently, stakeholder theory is, with the blessing of Ackoff (1919–2009), a concrete theory which enables corporations to represent themselves and to act on their environment. As such it functions on two levels: as corporate strategy and business strategy.

Representations of the Corporation in Strategic Management and the Emergence of Stakeholder Theory (1980–1990)

Over the course of the years, the discipline of strategic management has gradually constructed a representation of the corporation and of the legitimacy of its action. The various representations of the corporation proposed in the field of strategic management outline power relations that fashion legitimacy (Martinet and Reynaud 2001) and which, rather than being associated with a specific, all-powerful industrialist, are linked to negotiations with public opinion and institutions (legal, social, political). Following A.-C. Martinet (1990), the following schema outlines the evolution of those representations and traces the emergence of stakeholder theory.

Between 1950 and 1968, an Economistic Approach to the Corporation

Due to the financial demands of shareholders, the objectives of corporations were economic reconstruction, expansion and an emphasis on growth. Within the corporation, the gap between leaders and led was wide, and clashes between bosses and unions were harsh.

1968 and 1985: Strategic Representations of the Corporation

In the period situated between the euphoric crisis of 1968 and the globalization of the mid-1980s, multiple strategic representations of the corporation emerged. Monetarism and its guru, Milton Friedman, who asserted that the corporation should almost exclusively meet the expectations of society by "serving the interests of shareholders as effectively as possible" (1962), was called into question. A number of approaches to the organizational *design* of corporations emerged, with global enterprises and firms based on the idea that "small is beautiful" existing side-by-side. Between 1968 and 1985, emphasis was placed on strategic visions of the organization, with its fundamental choices constituting the corporation's *raison d'être*, an approach which ran counter to the financial vision which, according to Martinet, was largely indifferent to the substantial content of the firm's choices: What activities? What products? What clients?

1985 and 1995: A Financial Vision Combined with Multi-Criteria Performance and a Conception Offering an Alternative to Financial Orthodoxy

Two contradictory tendencies co-exist. On the one hand, preventive strategies concerning other firms and a substantial focus on shareholder value, and, on the other, an emphasis on societal performances and sustainable policies.

Since 1995: A Multitude of Different Perspectives

The leading model among those which have emerged since 1995 is based on an economy of knowledge and learning combined with the corporation's reactivity and ability to adopt simple, readily understandable rules governing their actions in the multiple channels of global distribution (Table 2.1).

Table 2.1 Another summary of currents in strategic management

Courants et écoles	Modèles représentatifs	Auteurs représentatifs	Observations
Design School de Harvard Corporate Strategy	SOWT (Forces, Faiblesses, Menaces, Opportunités)	Andrews équipe de Harvard 1960–1965	Approche rationnelle «conceptuelle» pour Mintzberg
Planification stratégique	Modèle de planification	Ansoff Ackoff 1965–1975	Approche systématique et analytique «formelle» pour Mintzberg
Business Strategy Stratégies opérationnelle Marketing stratégique	Modèles de portefeuille Modèles de positionnement Stratégies génériques	Levitt, Kotler Henderson 1965–1980 Abell	Grilles, check lists Processus «analytique» pour Mintzberg
Management stratégique	Domaines d'activités stratégiques	Hofer et Schendel 1978	
Stratégies de développement	Modèles de croissance: Économiques, financiers, organisationnels, etc.	Ansoff, Marris, Penrose 1960–1970	Forte diversité des approches. Non mentionné par Mintzberg
Courant environnemental	Modèles d'économie et d'organisation industrielles Approche évolutionniste Transaction	Porter 1975–1990 Nelson, Winter 1980–1990 Williamson 1975–1990	Conflit entre les approaches déductive (déterministers) et empiriques (contingentes) qualifié de « processus passif » (?) par Mintzberg
Courant organisationnel	Modèle de capacitiés Modèles contingents Transaction (interne) et économie des organisations	Mintzberg Lawrence et Lorsch Chandler, Cyert et March 1960–1990	Grande diversité des approches. Mintzberg retient l'approche « politique » et « culturelle »
Courant décisionnel	Modèle IMC et heuristique de la décision. Processus de prise de decision individueks et organisationnels	Simon et Mintzberg Crozier 1955–1990	Aproche empirique. Mintzberg distingue les approches «cognitives» et «d'apprentissage»
Courant entrepreneurial	Typologies d'entrepreneurs	Smith, Gasse 1960–1990	Approche typologique Processus « visionnaire »

Source: Marchesnay M, *Management stratégique* (2002: 38)

Translation

Currents and schools	Representative models	Representative authors	Observations
Harvard Design School Corporate strategy	SWOT (Strengths, Weaknesses, Opportunities, Threats)	Andrews' team at Harvard (1960–1965)	For Mintzberg, a rational, "conceptual" approach
Strategic planning	Planning model	Ansoff, Ackoff 1965–1975	Systematic, analytical approach, "formal" for Mintzberg
Business strategy	Portfolio model	Levitt, Kotler	Grids, check lists
Operational strategies	Position-based models	Henderson 1965–1980	For Mintzberg, an
Strategic marketing	Generic strategies	Abell	"analytical" process
Strategic management	Strategic fields of activity	Hofer and Schendel	
Development strategies	Growth models: economic, financial, organizational, etc.	Ansoff, Marris, Penrose 1960–1970	Wide range of approaches, not mentioned by Mintzberg
Environmental current	Economic, organizational industrial models	Porter 1975–1990	Conflict between deductive (determinist) and empirical (contingent) approaches described by Mintzberg as "passive [?] processes"
		Nelson, Winter 1980–1990	
		Williamson 1975–1990	
Organizational current	Capacities model Contingent models (Internal) transactions and economy of organizations	Mintzberg Lawrence and Lorsch Chandler, Cyert and March 1960–1990	Wide range of approaches Mintzberg retains the "political" and cultural approach
Decional current	IMC model and heurist decision-making. Individual and organizational decision-making processes	Simon and Mintzberg Crozier 1955–1990	Empirical approach. Mintzberg distinguishes between "cognitive" and "learning" approaches
Entrepreneurial current	Entrepreneurial typologies	Smith, Gasse 1960–1990	Typological approach

The Role of Stakeholder Theory in Corporate Strategy

The Corporation Between Dependence on the Environment and Policy Self-Determination

As a discipline, strategic management evolved from general corporate policy or "corporate strategy" (1908–1959) to strategic planning, or "corporate planning" (1960–1969) to "business strategy" (1970–1979). But it was in the 1980s that it became established as "an object of research in the sense of autonomous practices and normative prescriptions" (Laroche 2007). Stakeholder theory was at the heart of a number of currents and controversies within strategic management. In effect, it was defined both as a field of research within strategic management (an explicative framework of the environment) and as a toolbox for managers (a map of stakeholders providing a model of the competitive advantage of a firm on a particular market and determining its capacities for negotiation. It also reintroduced the possibility of corporate policy and of the prescriptive role of the corporation vis-à-vis public organizations and associations. Indeed, for corporate policy, stakeholders are a constrictive factor in terms of the strategy of the firm. In sum, the theory is located at the heart of strategic management (as is witnessed by the title of Freeman's 1984 book), since it is based on the most operational level of the corporation and seeks an improved articulation between the group as a whole and each of its product-market divisions. The theory's flexibility prompted a number of different interpretations within the field of strategy. For some authors, it encourages a "regeneration of strategy by means of the positive and normative actualization of policy in terms of ethics, styles of governance, responsibilities and operational approaches" (Martinet 2006). In the view of others, Freeman and his co-authors were thinking less about the frameworks of strategy and more about liberating managers from Porter's competitive approach and Pfeffer and Salancik's resource dependence theory (RDT) (Aggeri 2008). Furthermore, it has often been suggested that stakeholder theory is an alternative to a restrictive conception of strategy focusing on relations between managers and shareholders (agency theory) (Fig. 2.1).

These interpretations address the dilemma within strategy involving the choice between a deterministic and a proactive approach, a dilemma reflected in the famous debate, which took place in Pittsburgh in 1978, between, on the one hand, Ansoff and his content-based analysis, and, on the other, Pettigrew and his process-based approach (Dery 1996). However, when stakeholder theory emerged in the 1980s it was influenced by both content-based and process-based approaches in strategy. Moreover, stakeholder theory is still an object of debate in corporate strategy between authors who advocate a relatively deterministic and adaptive vision (a descriptive stance which accords great importance to questions of positioning and the implementation of strategy), and scholars who support a more voluntaristic and proactive approach (a prescriptive stance encouraging strategic prescription).

Stakeholder Theory: Promoting Strategic Management, 1970–1980

In terms of the evolution of strategic currents, the strategic planning of the 1960s and 1970s gave way to the strategic management of the 1970s–1990s.

Strategic planning is often confused with the development of plans and the implementation of budgetary procedures. The plan, a general policy tool, is used for

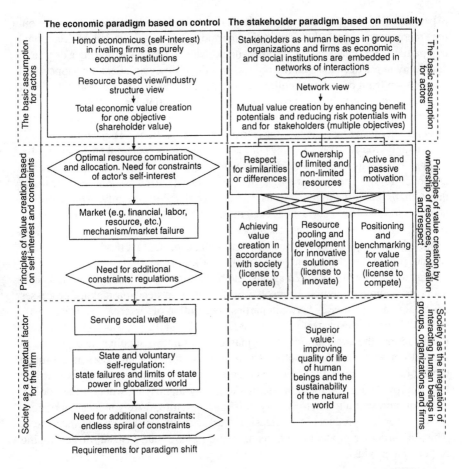

Fig. 2.1 Comparison between the economic paradigm and the stakeholder paradigm (Source: Sachs S. and Ruhli E., *Stakeholders Matter: A New Paradigm for Strategy in Society* (2011: 76))

predicting (fixing objectives, organizing resources) and monitoring (ensuring that objectives are met). In the 1970s, corporations in mass consumer goods industries were faced with a decline in the market. This decline prefigured trade competitiveness problems between 1975 and 1985 and, later, in the second decade of the third millennium. As early as 1984, strategic planning no longer exactly corresponded to the needs of large companies in which strategy was situated on two levels: the ensemble, or group (corporate strategy) and individual product-market divisions (business strategy).

In the period in which globalization first took hold, corporate strategy was criticized on two grounds: first, because planning pre-supposed a stable and predictable environment, while conditions were increasingly less stable and predictable; moreover, activities, including operational activities, are permanently subject to strategic thinking and adapted, on a day-to-day basis, to new external factors (the expectations of clients and suppliers, the perception of strong or weak signals about the emergence of new technologies). Furthermore, during this period, multinational companies were organized into product-market divisions, thus acquiring a degree of autonomy in the decision-making process (product life-cycle). Seeking support and information from operational collaborators, strategic management was applied first and foremost to unstable contexts characterized by continuous change. Thus, strategy was not defined once and for all for a 3- or 5-year period but *continuously* through successive approximations, errors and corrections. The *corporate* level increasingly focused on the ways in which decisions were taken at all levels. Second, *corporate* and *business* aspects were combined and articulated (Hofer and Schendel 1996). The term strategic management was used because it is in fact a question of coordinating decisions characterized by uncertainty. The approach attempts to establish a correspondence between global aims and fields of strategic activity. Third, *corporate* and *business* strategy increasingly focused on market expectations. Emphasis was placed on marketing aspects; first product-market, and second, product-market-technology (Abell 1980).

Stakeholder theory emerged against the backdrop of the kind of issues that strategic management attempts to resolve by focusing on decision-making processes and negotiation processes between parties. The notion of "internal" and "external" stakeholders became centrally important (Figs. 2.2 and 2.3). It was applied in order to ensure that the expectations of the market, consumers, suppliers and publics in general corresponded to the offer. Consequently, stakeholder theory is useful in terms of strategic marketing. However, an original aspect of the theory is that it is able to provide a guide for strategic marketing by identifying what, in the market, does not represent a threat to society. It is not, therefore, merely a question of constantly renewing products, or increasing market share, or anticipating the time at which a particular product enters its saturation phase, but, instead, of developing responsible products.

A Pluralist Representation of the Corporation and of the Organization: Toward Partnership-Based Corporate Governance

We have already highlighted the fact that stakeholder theory was, above all, an alternative to the orthodox, or rather, monist, theory of corporate governance according to which the corporation is a contractual relationship between shareholders and directors (Jensen and Meckling 1976; Shleifer and Vishny 1997). Although alternative, stakeholder theory has sometimes been reduced to a dual relationship between shareholders and non-shareholders. But value also depends on cooperation (Aoki 1984) not only between stakeholders, shareholders and directors, but also creditors, employees, suppliers and public authorities.

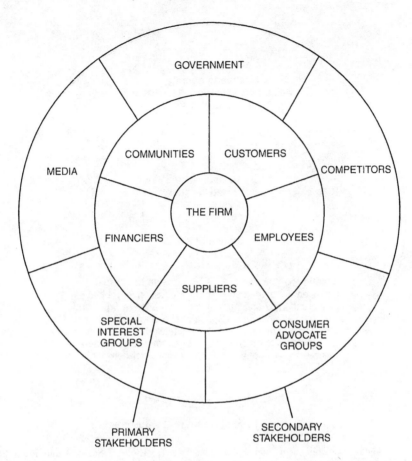

Fig. 2.2 The stakeholder wheel (1984–2007) (Source: R. Edward Freeman, Jeffrey S. Harrison, and Andrew C. Wicks, *Managing for Stakeholders: Survival, Reputation, and Success* (2007), New Haven: Yale University Press)

Freeman made a major contribution to changing approaches to corporate governance (Freeman and Reed 1983; Freeman and Evan 1990). Other authors have supported him, notably Cornell and Shapiro (1987), who compared the advantages of a corporate model based on stakeholders with a financial model. Indeed, in terms of research into strategic and financial management, shareholders have gradually lost their primacy to stakeholders (Caby 2003) since, if all individual categories of stakeholders have their expectations vis-à-vis the corporation, it is because each one of them contributes, or believes that they contribute to value creation. However, one current of the French school of management science – G. Charreaux, P. Desbrières, P-Y Gomez, F Parrat, J.M. Plane, P. Wirtz – paints a less utopian picture than Freeman's of the rootedness of stakeholders in corporate governance (Table 2.2).

Charreaux and Desbrières have worked since 1998 on developing a method for measuring and maximizing partnership value with a view to promoting a pluralist

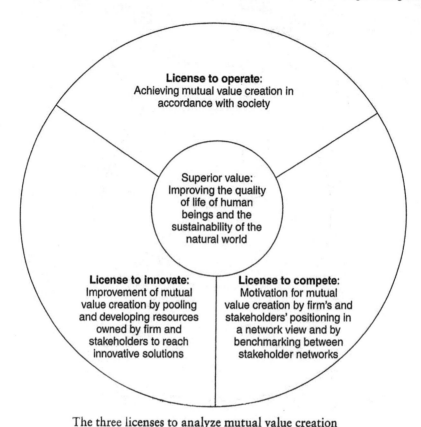

The three licenses to analyze mutual value creation

Fig. 2.3 Another version of the stakeholder wheel (2011) (Source: Sachs S and Rühli E, *Stakeholders Matter: A New Paradigm for Strategy in Society* (2011: 83))

vision of the corporation. In 1999, Parrat (1999) published an overview of the various contributions of stakeholders. He defined value creation as the difference between opportunity costs for the client and the sum of opportunity costs for partners as a whole (clients, suppliers, shareholders, employees, directors). In the traditional financial approach, the value created is equal to the rent received by shareholders. Partnership value measurement is based on the overall measurement of the rent generated by the corporation in relation to the various stakeholders (Charreaux and Wirtz 2006). The authors highlight a form of managerial slack, or, in other words, an excess representing the leeway enjoyed by the director in his or her negotiations with various partners. This "slack," which is not shared by all the stakeholders, is reinvested or conserved in the form of liquidities. What distinguishes the pluralist view of Charreaux and Desbrières from Freeman's perspective is that Freeman specifically calls for corporate democracy (Freeman and Reed 1983), while the French partnership value current is situated in a normative perspective of corporate governance informed by the objective of guaranteeing the viability of coalitions favoring wealth creation (Charreaux 1997).

Table 2.2 Typology of strategies in function of relationships between stockholders and stakeholders

<u>**Narrow Stakeholder Strategy**</u>

Maximize benefits to one or a small set of stakeholders

<u>**Stockholder Strategy**</u>

Maximize benefits to stockholders

Maximize benefits to «financial stakeholders»

<u>**Utilitarian Strategy**</u>

Maximize benefits to all stakeholders (greatest good for greatest number)

Maximize average welfare level of all stakeholders

Maximize benefits to society

<u>**Rawisian Strategy**</u>

Act to raise the level of the worst-off stakeholder

<u>**Social Harmony Strategy**</u>

Act to maintain or create social harmony

Act to gain consensus from society

Source: R. E. Freeman, *Strategic Management* (1984: 102)

Strategic Models Which Are Not Congruent with Stakeholder Theory: Michael Porter

Michael Porter's Competitive Advantage

While stakeholder theorists attempted to make a breakthrough in strategic management, Michael Porter's theory of competitive advantage, elaborated in his books *Competitive Strategy* (1980) and *Competitive Advantage* (1985) was recognized by many managers, consultants and academics as THE leading theory in the field. Even today, Porter's competitive advantage is a dominant model in management strategy, as if all thinking in the field had come to an end in 1985. Competitive advantage was a development of the LCAG model (Learned et al. 1965), which gave rise to SWOT analysis (Strength, Weakness, Opportunity, Threat). In an approach based on the product-market relationship, Porter asks how a corporation can seek to achieve a quasi-monopolistic position, thus guaranteeing substantial levels of profit. In his view, corporations have a permanent objective, namely to increase their size, and, consequently, negotiating power and economies of scale by boosting production and thereby decreasing marginal costs. In fact, the more product the corporation produces, the less the unit cost will be. To the LCAG model, which diagnoses the corporation on the basis of its market share and its rate of growth in a specific sector with a view to managing a portfolio of areas of activity, Porter adds five forces competing with the SWOT model: (1) rivalry between competitors in the market; (2) clients' negotiating power (demand for a reduction in cost price and, consequently, a reduction in margins); (3) suppliers' negotiating power (demand for an increase in sale price and thus a reduction in the firm's margins); (4) the threat represented by substitute products, and, (5) potential entrants on the market. Commentators talk of competitive advantage when a firm has the capacity to increase its negotiating power vis-à-vis suppliers and clients and, therefore, vis-à-vis competitors. Nevertheless, this kind of negotiation is based on a simple dominant-dominated relationship and not on a relationship between parties who are potentially equal in terms of the pressure they are able to exert.

In spite of an efficient conceptual framework (the industrial structure influences the rules of the competitive game and the strategies potentially available to the firm), the theory has been criticized on a number of grounds. The environment is presented in a fragmentary manner: only the industrial structure of the sector in which the firm in question operates is taken into account, while convergence phenomena between industries are neglected. Relationships between firms are exclusively competitive, as are relationships between large companies and small enterprises, and between clients and suppliers. Porter thus confines himself to the market environment, or, in other words, to a standard representation based on a belief in a kind of pure and perfect, monopolistic or oligopolistic from of competition (Marchesnay 2002).

Stakeholder theory provides a broader vision of the strategic environment by encompassing factors that are not purely competitive. It focuses on the articulation between the structural parameters of the macro-environment and the corporation, while at the same taking into account the role of institutions, regulations, the emergence of new actors, and the impact of technological breakthroughs. Above all, stakeholder theory refutes the idea that relations between competitors are merely hierarchical. It describes an environment characterized by an increasing number of relations and, consequently, a potentially infinite number of interactions. To relations with clients and suppliers are added relations with economic, political and administrative institutions at various levels. This is why Freeman (2010) suggests that Porter's well known value chain should include the stakeholders who compose it. In this regard, Porter himself believes in the value of an enriched representation of the strategic environment no longer exclusively made up of competitors, a viewpoint he expresses in *The Competitive Advantage of Corporate Philanthropy* (Porter and Kramer 2002) and "Creating Shared Value" (Porter and Kramer 2011). In effect, the concept of "shared value" means implies that the corporation should meet vital social needs (health, habitat, care, environment) that can be described in terms of stakeholder theory. It should be acknowledged that the strength of the theory to which Porter has partially rallied is its emphasis on the corporation's dependence on its multiple relations with other entities. This aspect of the theory differs from numerous currents in strategy and management for which entrepreneurship is a relatively autonomous activity (Fig. 2.4).

In spite of these rapprochements, it is unlikely that stakeholder theory will ever be entirely appropriated by the competitive advantage perspective. Other currents have more in common with stakeholder theory, including the relational view (Dyer and Singh 1998) and the coopetition model (Brandenburger and Nalebuff 1995). To

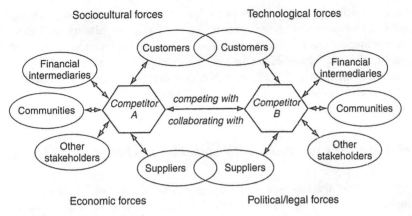

Competing stakeholder networks
Note: The overlapping ovals are an indication that competitors are likely to share some of the same customers and suppliers. We acknowledge that overlaps may also occur with other types of stakeholders as well.

Fig. 2.4 Competing stakeholder networks (Source: R. E. Freeman and al, *Stakeholder Theory. The State of the Art*, Cambridge University Press (2010: 118))

paraphrase these last we could say that: "making the biggest cake is cooperation; sharing it is competition" (quoted by Desreumaux et al. 2006).

According to the coopetition model developed by Bradenburger and Nalebuff (1995), competition is compatible with selective cooperative projects, including, in terms of products, substitutes (substituor) and complements (complementor) that are relative values. More concretely, in coopetition, the type of behavior to be adopted in regard to "S"s and "C"s is a choice (linked to the creation or capture of value). For example, Lancôme and Estée Lauder are substitutes from the point of view of their customers. The concept of "S" is more wide-ranging than that of the direct competitor. The "C"s are firms from whom clients buy complementary products or to whom suppliers sell complementary resources. This relationship makes it possible to describe the interdependence of certain sectors, something that Porter has found it hard to do. Recourse to the concepts of "S" and "C" makes it possible to identify certain organizations, interdependent vis-à-vis a given firm, which create or recuperate the value associated with that firm. The value created is greater than the interactions outlined in the value chain.

Richard D'Aveni's Hyper-Competition Model (1994–2010)

To talk about hypercompetition is to describe an economic context in which competitive advantages such as cost, price, time, quality, technological advantages, innovation and funding have been replaced by ephemeral and variable combinations. Richard D'Aveni writes of an "age of temporary advantage" (2010). "Strategy is no longer based on the construction of sustainable advantages, but on the art of continually challenging the *status quo*: speed and aggression in terms of action taken, multiple initiatives, a constant modification of the rules of the game and arenas of competition is the leitmotiv of competitors who spend a great deal of time imitating one another" (Desreumaux et al. 2006).

Strategic Models Compatible with Stakeholder Theory

As is by now clear, the emergence and development of stakeholder theory took place against a backdrop of multiple strategic theories elaborated in response to the globalization of trade and profound transformations in private organizations. In the words of Franck Aggeri (2008), an attempt was made to "regenerate the frameworks of strategy." The author adds: "To the different Porterian, post-Porterian and anti-Porterian currents, should be added approaches to strategy applying a multi-level reading (Pettigrew, Mintzberg) based on a collective construction of meaning (Weick 1995), or on an institutional construction of meaning (Desreumaux 2004; Hualt 2004) implying the *in situ* application of cognitive resources" (Aggeri 2008). Some approaches are strikingly congruent with stakeholder theory, particularly the French current led by Jarniou (1981) and Martinet (1984), which developed the work of Tabatoni and Jarniou (1975). This current was pursued by Baron in Quebec (1995). Its advocates' intention is to deconstruct the deterministic aspects of corporate policy or, in other words, to rethink corporate strategy. At the same time, R.E. Freeman (1984) in the United States, and A.-C. Martinet in France developed the foundations of an alternative corporate strategy. Another model, this one based on the work of Edith Penrose (1959), developed by Birger Wernerfelt (1984) and J.B. Barney (1989) came to challenge Porterian orthodoxy in the 1990s.

The Corporation as a Political System: The Francophone School of 1980–2009

The Corporation as the Fundamental Unit of Social Organization A site of production and work, the corporation is a source of creativity and wealth. It has become common to consider it as a fundamental organization within society (Hafsi and Martinet 2007; Gomez and Korine 2009; Aymard-Duvernay 2004) in the same way as other institutions. The fact that external actors demand that it meets expectations previously associated with the public good is a symptom of major institutional changes. In effect, the corporation is located at the heart of displacements of legitimate and political powers, of the emergence of new organizations which are neither public nor private (see Part 3). The legitimacy of the sovereign entities that are the nation-states was long based on the exclusive right to exercise political authority (legislative, legal and executive) in a given geographical area or over a give population. This legitimacy persists, but is now counterbalanced by organizations already located on a level that is at once regional and international. Thus, international organizations, for example the European Union, possess some degree of sovereignty due to their substantial legislative competencies in highly strategic areas such as energy, the environment, chemicals and agriculture, in which it passes between 60 and 70% of new legislation To this it should be added that, in most of the EU, trade is conducted in a single currency, the euro. The erosion of national public legitimacies can above all be observed in three regards: *first*, the development of the activity of international organizations (IOs), principally those which exist to promote inter-state coordination. As well as international organization designed to defend the interests of major geographical regions like the Association of Southeast Nations (ASEAN), there are also international organizations whose mission is to reduce the level of global economic disparities, like the EBRD (European Bank for Reconstruction and Development), the Ibrd (International Bank for Reconstruction and Development), and the IDB (Inter-American Development Bank). *Second*, the development of inter-governmental organizations (IGOs), for example, the WTO, as well as organizations like the IFAD (International Fund for Agricultural Development), the IMF (International Monetary Fund), the ICAO (International Civil Aviation Organization), the ILO (International Labor Organization), and the UNITAR (United Nations Institute for Training and Research). *Third*, non-governmental organizations (NGOs). *Fourth*, multinational companies which are powerful actors, since most political organizations are either limited to a specific territory (the nation-state) or are under construction. Moreover, multinationals possess human resources quantitatively superior to most public administrations of nation-states and their turnover figures are often higher than the GDP of some countries. We believe that, confronted with multinational organizations that are over a 100 years old, most regional organizations are still under development. This is true of the EU. Private organizations, particularly very large companies, negotiate directly not only with all these organizations (IOs, IGOs, NGOs), but also with the individuals who either affect or are affected by them.

The Political Firm The idea of a political company was very far from familiar, either to members of the public or to members of the academic community when, in 1981, Pierre Jarniou published *L'entreprise comme système politique*, which followed in the wake of the sociologist and economist, Pierre Tabatoni (Tabatoni and Jarniou 1975). These authors advance the idea of a crisis of legitimacy of public institutions (Laufer and Paradeise 1982). Researchers in strategic management, Alain-Charles Martinet in France (1984), and Jean Pasquero in Quebec (1980, 2008), underline the importance of describing the social and societal environment. Alongside competitive forces, alongside the structural variables of change, be they societal (demographic evolution), political (new regulations), economic (interest rates, exchange rates), competitive (the impact of new technologies, price variations, new products), or market-related (new product uses, new markets), an increasing number of socio-political pressures are emerging in the shape of demands made on the corporation by specific sectors of society. These last generate new social costs, generally borne by the corporation's production activities. Beyond the Francophone world, other researchers have applied similar hypotheses and come to similar conclusions (Preston and Post 1975; David P. Baron 1995, 2006). Baron underlines the importance of non-market strategies, particularly the 4Is, namely "issues", or questions to be resolved; "interests"; "institutions", or relevant institutional actors; and "information" to which the corporation has only partial access. Corporate policy includes lobbying, or efforts by groups of activists to control market opportunities, as distinct from market strategy, which focuses on the relationship between products and markets. In this sense, there is a political aspect to strategy corresponding to the corporation's political strategies. Thus, while the corporation is often presented as a technico-economic unit or a local social organization, stakeholder theory presents it as "an entity in a political space" (Martinet 1984, 2006). Much more than this, the corporation is transformed into a specific institution.

Resource and Skills-Based Strategy

While Porter's competitive analysis was sweeping all before it, a less deterministic model, focusing on the specificities of the firm rather than on the sector in which it operated, emerged in the wake of research carried out by Edith Penrose. This model is based on resources and skills. Instead of emphasizing growth in terms of size, proponents of the approach focus on exploiting and intensifying the corporation's main skills and resources, leaving other activities to partners or sub-contractors. Resources in this context include not only human resources, but also raw materials, labor, capital, equipment, knowledge and market opportunities for products and services. Resources include tangible and intangible assets possessed by a firm that enable it to determine its strategy and improve its performance. Managers must envisage ways of counterbalancing the firm's dependence on its resources.

Stakeholder theory is close to Barnay's model in a number of respects: first, because it focuses on a sustainable competitive advantage that is not exclusively constituted by business opportunities; and second, because its value is based on resources. This unique combination of the firm's skills and resources associated with their intrinsic characteristics is at the origin of competitive advantage. Because skills are rare, they are strategic; they can only be imperfectly imitated by existing or potential competitors. Such skills are hard to exchange because they are the result of a long individual and collective learning process that integrates the knowledge and aptitudes of individuals, specific kinds of management, values, norms, and the way in which knowledge is monitored.

In *Stakeholder Theory: The State of the Art*, Freeman et al. (2010: 95) recognize that "resource-based and stakeholder perspectives are complementary rather than competing [even though] the links between stakeholder theory and the resource-based view have not been adequately established in the minds of many strategic management scholars." In effect, the firm is also dependent on the resources acquired from its stakeholder network.

The Relational View

Freeman et al. (2010: 108) claim that the relational view is an extension of stakeholder theory. In effect, Dyer and Singh (1998: 661) underline the importance of routines and processes in networks as a source of competitiveness. In this regard, inter-organizational relationships take center stage. This model is based on research on partnerships, joint-projects and alliances that can improve performance by reducing costs and risks, as well as by increasing value for clients. The cooperative relationship takes the form of a partnership, increasing potential for relations based on reciprocal trust as a gauge of performance. The relationship is defined by a collective approach to problem-solving; the sharing of knowledge (particularly tacit knowledge); the reduction of uncertainty associated with business relations; the development of a common language; the acceptance of routines reducing transaction costs; and the shared quest for a satisfactory price with a view to safeguarding the relationship rather than focusing on maximizing profits. Negotiation is about more than just the economic criterion of price. For Freeman too, the concept of the relationship assumes a strategic aspect, especially when it is associated with negotiation. In effect, the agendas of company directorates contain issues which do not concern them directly, but on which they are asked to express their opinions: questions of a socio-political order encompassing issues such as the status of minorities (recruitment, skills and career development), ecological movements, the decline of unionism, and the legitimacy of negotiations. To this can be added the emergence of new actors, as in Brandenburger and Nalebuff's model. Stakeholder theory could be applied to substitutes (*substitutor*) and complements (*complementor*), thus relativizing the importance of central actors.

Impact of Stakeholder Theory on Strategic Marketing and Research in Negotiation

In strategic marketing, the notion of the dependence of the corporation on its environment has not escaped the attention of researchers active in the field who deal with the multiple links between the firm and its customs, suppliers, manufacturers and distributors (Kotler 2005). A number of marketing researchers take an interest in stakeholder theory (Roper and Davies 2007; Miller and Lewis 1991). The corporation creates value not only for itself, but also for specific clients, whose expectations and the levels of performance required to satisfy it attempts to define. The value created by the corporation is derived from the modification of its initial strategy and the emergence of a degree of empathy between prospects and clients on the one hand, and the brand on the other. Christopher et al. (1991) describe a six markets framework (the customer market, the referral market – or, in other words, the market of consumers recommending the corporation –, the influence market, the supplier market, the recruitment market, and the firm's own internal market. Whatever the case, thanks to this new approach, the corporation has more options at its disposal and more opportunities to create value (Colla 2011). Nevertheless, stakeholder theory is used in other ways in marketing, for example to analyze customer resistance and develop strategies to take it into account (Holt 2002; Heath and Potter 2004; Roux 2007).

The vast field of negotiation associated with management research (international strategy and management, strategic marketing, human resources), as well as political science and the sociology of politics, also bear witness to the theory's robust character. In effect, if stakeholder theory aims at consensus, why bring up issues, rights and interests? In short, why negotiate? It has often been suggested that stakeholder theory avoids the idea of conflict by positing a necessary conciliation between market and society. Although a number of studies on negotiation focus on joint research on mutual gains (the Harvard School), the diversity of approaches to negotiation and their applications (in international relations, political science, social relations, sales management, law and psychology) suggests that research in negotiation would considerably enrich the theory.

Such a development would shift the emphasis from an integrative perspective (integrating stakeholders) to a generative one (Thuderoz 2010). In effect, for many researchers, conflicts – considered as interactions – can be either constructive or destructive (Senghaas 1973; Krippendorf 1973). Indeed, serve to differentiate various positions, intentions and interests (Fisher and Ury 1981; Susskind 2000).

Conclusion

The advocates of stakeholder theory have always claimed that its origins are to be sought in strategic management. In this section, we have examined the most important currents in the discipline, both those with which stakeholder theory has a number of affinities, and those with which it is not congruent. Some of these currents are seen as extensions of the theory, while others are regarded as complementary to it. Indeed, some authors, for example Sachs and Rühli (2011), see the theory as a new paradigm in strategic management that redefines the corporation and the organization (Post et al. 2002). In entrepreneurship, it is possible to demonstrate that activity is not only dependent on groups or individuals, but also on rules implied by legislation and norms. In this regard, stakeholder theory is similar to neo-institutionalism.

In order to enter this paradigm, it is necessary to move beyond an exclusively economic model based on the maximization of profit and take into account the wealth, diversity and complexity of the social dynamics surrounding and affecting the corporation. In this sense, stakeholder theory is congruent with the view of Gioia and Pitre (1990), for whom strategic management is deployed in a multitude of perspectives. Far from being an obstacle to the measurement of corporate performance, stakeholder theory proposes multi-level performance criteria which presuppose a long-term vision (Freeman et al. 2010: 117). Nevertheless, for most authors associated with the theory, the integration of stakeholders implies a cognitive revolution in the corporation and its structure (Gersick 1991), as well as in its instances of governance, and its decision-making and learning processes.

Chapter 3
Stakeholder Theory as a Theory of Organizations

There have been so many studies on organization between the 1980s and 2010, borrowing from so many different sources, that it would be vain to attempt to demonstrate how stakeholder theory has attempted to appropriate or influence any given model. Nevertheless, 30 years were needed to jettison the evolutionist notion of the "one best way" in organization studies, a notion that can be traced from Max Weber to Henry Mintzberg. Stakeholder theory has contributed to this process of deconstruction. In effect, systemic approaches (other than Gestalt theory and theories related to Michel Crozier's "concrete action system") have cast the organization, and particularly the corporation, as an ensemble of independent parties articulated with a single objective in mind. Thus, the vast majority of studies produced in the field of organization studies have promoted an essentialist view of an entity focused on its own mode of functioning, describing a structure centered on determinants (Mintzberg 1979, 1983; Mintzberg et al. 1998). In this regard, the objectifiable and finite character of the organization suggests "a coordinating entity with identifiable frontiers functioning in a sustainable manner while at the same time attempting to achieve one or more objectives shared by the participants" (Robbins 1987). But structure is not appropriate to a fluid (and fundamentally plastic) conception of the organization based on stakeholders. Far from being a fortress founded on structural determinants, the organization is porous. And stakeholder theory dispenses with the biological and engineering foundations of systemic analysis, reconstructing the approach on properly managerial and political bases. With stakeholder theory, the study of organizations turns its attention to the notions of interest, the negotiation of issues, and the management of more or less stable relations both within and outside the organization. In this sense, the organization is a kind of "collectivity sharing one or more common interests and engaging in shared activities." It is thus "a coalition of groups with variable interests which elaborates objectives by means of negotiation" (Scott 1987).

© The Author(s) 2016
M. Bonnafous-Boucher, J.D. Rendtorff, *Stakeholder Theory*, SpringerBriefs in
Ethics, DOI 10.1007/978-3-319-44356-0_3

Stakeholder Theory, a Factor of Change in Organization Theory

The French tradition of organization theory is generally more closely associated with the sociology than with the economics of organizations (Chabaud et al. 2008). It is relatively untouched by the fruitful debates on organization studies carried out between 1980 and 2000 by economists, sociologists, psycho-sociologists and linguists, who chose to study the process of organizing rather than the organization as an entity. However, a number of research projects have radically altered the field. One thinks, of course, of the work of C. Casey (2002), of S. R. Clegg (1979, 1981, 1996), and R. Westwood and S. R. Clegg (2003) not only on rules and monitoring, but also on the extra-organizational aspects of organizations. One thinks also of the neo-institutionalism of W. W. Powell and P. J. DiMaggio (1991) and of W. R. Scott (1995); of the work of K. E. Weick and D. A. Gioia (1986) on the construction of meaning in small groups; of the work of Granovetter (1985), Tsoukas and Knudsen (2003), and Brunsson and Goran (2008) – introduced into France by Dumez (the *Le Libellio* of the Ecole Polytechnique's Management Research Center, 2005–2011) – on incomplete organizations and meta-organizations; of the work of A. Strati (1999) on the power of form in organizations; of the work of Nicolini et al. (2003), for whom organizing is an activity which creates an indissociable link between doing and knowing. But the French approach to organization theory sometimes produces an erratic image of itself and tends to focus on autonomous entities, considering the organization as an ensemble or a system (an approach which makes it hard to describe complex external situations). It is hardly necessary to recall that the systemic analysis inherited from Bertalanffy (1951) and Lussato (1977) describes an ensemble made up of inter-dependent sub-systems. This approach was used to emphasize the importance of internal coordination mechanisms on the structure of the organization (Mintzberg 1979). But in spite of its remarkable contributions to the discipline, the approach nevertheless fostered a dichotomy between private and public organizations, and under-estimated the impact of the internationalization of the economy and commercial trade on both private and public organizations, and on the creation of new organizations in the interstices between the public and private sectors (international organizations, public organizations with a global vocation). The growth of hybrid organizations combining objectives of a public and private order has also been under-estimated, as has the importance of competitiveness clusters operating in regional or national spheres and informed by global aspirations: exporting innovation from one country to the rest of the world (Figs. 3.1 and 3.2).

Stakeholder theory veers away from an exclusive emphasis on structural determinants by embedding the organization within companies and markets and by temporalizing that embeddedness. Stakeholder theory has the effect of altering the perspective of organization studies, obliging its practitioners to take new factors

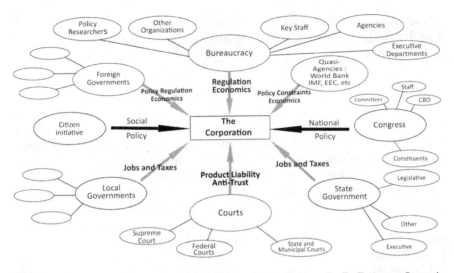

Fig. 3.1 An example of a representation of complexity (Source: R. E. Freeman, *Strategic Management, A Stakeholder Approach* (1984))

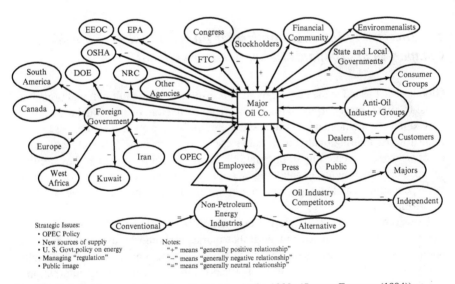

Fig. 3.2 Stakeholders map of a major oil company in the 1980s (*Source*: Freeman (1984))

into account, namely, (1). the increasing number of private and public global orga-nizations; (2). the emergence of hybrid organizations; and (3). the importance of issues concerning inter-organizational coordination, agreements, regulations and negotiation.

From Structure to Its Fragmentation:
The Internationalization of Organizations and of Inter-organizational Relations

In stakeholder theory, the environment is often represented as a core (the firm) surrounded by a constellation of stakeholders. It is true that the schematic nature of this representation has come in for a substantial amount of criticism. But the remarkable thing about such schemas is not that they identify stakeholders, albeit in an approximative manner, within society. Since the 1980s, research has no longer focused exclusively on the internal coordination of manufacturing-type organizations, but has also taken into account non-hierarchical (network) coordination between organizations whose missions are international and whose objectives are often very distinct in commercial, strategic and political terms. However, such organizations share a common concern: the capacity to coordinate other entities or other actors in terms of transnational activities. These changes in scale of analysis are the result of at least three factors: the internationalization of private organizations; the growing number of international organizations with a regional or global vocation; and a profound transformation within public organizations.

The Increasing Internationalized of Firms: From Very Large Companies to Companies That Are Born Global

Global trade has led to the development of transnational and multinational organizations. In effect, most corporate functions are now linked to international trade. Even very small companies and medium-sized enterprises have not been spared by this trend toward internationalization: some companies are now "born global" or, in other words, are located in an international market from the moment they are first set up. This situation has engendered new kinds of demands on the part of collaborators, consumers and all those who are indirectly affected by the activities of these organizations.

However, the impact of internationalization on organizations, some or all of whose activities are carried out in global markets, should be examined from the point of view of the various phases of the process. Some organizations focus exclusively on export (selling to foreign markets), others are becoming international (producing and selling in limited areas abroad), and some are going global (with a worldwide presence guaranteed by their subsidiaries). These various approaches to the process of internationalization imply a range of different perspectives on organizational. Thus, given that export (selling products manufactured in a particular country in foreign markets) is often the beginning of the process of internationalization, one of these methods is export focusing on commercial trade networks. This approach can involve brokers, purchase divisions, "piggy tracking" (in which firms use the commercial services of larger companies to sell their products abroad), economic interest groups active in the export market, and sub-contractors. Legal proce-dures (licenses) are also used. In a more advanced phase, agents, customs officers, franchises, subsidiaries and joint-ventures are often more appropriate. Subsidiaries can take different forms; they can, for example, be commercial or integrated. Concessions represent another approach. Delocalization, or, in other words, the transference of activities to a country other than the one in which production ini-tially took place, is motivated by a desire to reduce production costs, be nearer to end consumers and sidestep customs levies. Lastly, multinationals are situated at the top end of the spectrum of commitment, control and organization. They produce and sell in the numerous countries in which they have subsidiaries. They take a global approach to financing strategy, production and distribution. They harmonize structures and procedures between countries, optimize localizations by region, inte-grate networks by transforming them into internal sub-contracting systems, and ensure that their IT systems are unique and centralized. Corporations choose to take this step in order to distribute risk, create economies of scale (reducing unit produc-tion costs by increasing the size of the production plant), and boost their negotiation potential.

The various actors in a transnational market are confronted by organizational issues of an entirely different order from those faced by manufacturing companies in the early twentieth century. Organization theory, therefore, not only deals with the determinants of internal structures but also attempts to describe and interpret inter- and intra-organizational relations, which are often framed within networks and which are not characterized by hierarchical links.

International Regulatory Organizations with a Global Vocation

Corporations are not the only organizations to have become internationalized; many public organizations have taken a similar course. The International Law Commission (ILC) defines an international organization as "any organization instituted by a treaty or other instrument governed by international law and equipped with its own international legal personality. An international organization can include amongst its members entities other than states." International organizations have a legal per-sonality distinct from that of member states. An international organization can be an association of sovereign states established by an agreement, or by an international treaty which defines its status. It is equipped with an apparatus of permanent, shared bodies. There are two types of international organization:

– International organizations with a global vocation such as the United Nations, the International Labor Organization (ILO), the International Atomic Energy Agency (IAEA), the World Health Organization (WHO), the European Organization for Nuclear Research (CERN), the Organization for Economic Co-Operation and Development (OECD), and the International Organization of

Legal Metrology (IOML). Some have a well-defined geographical field, for example the European Union, OPEC, the OECD and NATO.

- Non-Governmental Organizations. Currently, there are some 3000 NGOs around the world. In 1996, there were 320, and in 1950, only 100. Private law associations, and, as such, moral entities with an international scope, NGOs are associations which act in the public interest without being attached either to a state or to an international institution.

Public Organizations Undergoing Profound Changes

Public organizations are undergoing profound changes associated with the management of the public debt. For example, in France, the Incorporating Act relative to the Finance Laws of August 1, 2001, and the General Revision of Public Policy (or "RGPP" launched in 2007, and implemented in early 2009) have profoundly transformed the way in which public action is organized within structures tasked with non-commercial and commercial missions carried out in the public interest. Among the bodies impacted are government administrations, territorial authorities (regions, *départements, communes*), public administrative establishments (EPAs), public establishments of an industrial and commercial character (EPICs), and private law public commercial enterprises most of whose capital is supplied by the state.

In addition to these national organizations, public organizations with a global mission have also emerged – the WTO, the International Criminal Court, the International Monetary Fund, UNITAR (the United Nations Institute for Training and Research), and many others. Moreover, there are also a number of sector-based international organizations working in the public interest, including the International Development Agency, the International Fund for Agricultural Development, the International Civil Aviation Organization, as well as the European Bank for Reconstruction and Development and its international homologue, the International Bank for Reconstruction and Development, and the Inter-American Development Bank. Coordinating organizations such as ASEAN (Association of Southeast Asian Nations), whose mission is to defend the interests of major world regions, should also be taken into account. A number of the organizations listed above did not yet exist at the beginning of the twentieth century. All of them help define the historical conditions in which coordinating and regulating mechanisms can be implemented. They also provide competitive opportunities for the deployment organizational skills. That is why economists are so concerned with the role of international economic organizations in inter-governmental cooperation (Jacquet et al. 2002). A common theme of such economists is that the political regulation of globalization is based on the optimization – based on a distribution of tasks – of relations between international organizations, with the objective of developing a political model capable of guaranteeing the efficiency of inter-governmental institutions. The emphasis of organization theory thus shifts from the internal analysis of organizations to an examination of coordination and arbitrage in raw materials markets, and the division of labor among international organizations.

Stakeholder theory should make it possible to take into account three major factors in the transformation of organizations: the internationalization of private organizations; the growing number of international organizations; and the profound transformation undergone by public organizations. Consequently, it makes an active contribution to redefining the organization as an object of study within a broader environment. Thus, in terms of the concept of the environment, while it is true that states benefit from globalization, it cannot be said that they control it. Comprises are struck in the form of public, national, regional and international norms, as well as private norms. This intertwining of rules is the constant object of flexible negotiation. And the stability of the international system derives from a network of international regimes providing a permanent, organized (although unstable) framework for states. The paradigm of regimes useful for the analysis of international relations becomes pertinent in organization theory, with the "regime" consisting in "networks of rules, norms and procedures that regularize behavior and control its effects" (Keohane and Nye 1977). Within this framework, stakeholder theory is particularly appropriate in that one of the major currents of regime theory focuses on interests. In effect, as Chavagneux (2004) notes, regime theory is characterized by three major approaches (Hasenclever et al. 1983): (1) the interest-based approach regimes are the result of the interests of states; they generate the information required to reduce uncertainty and make cooperation possible; (2) the power-based approach (regimes result above all from the relative power of different states and are more stable when one of those states is in a dominant position); and (3) the knowledge-based approach (the way in which states define themselves in relation to one another and determine their interests depends on the normative beliefs and knowledge of decision-makers).

Organization Theory and Stakeholder Theory

Any examination of organization theory outside France would reveal, to use the phrase employed by Linda Rouleau (2007), that "heterodoxy is dominant." Attempting to take on board the diversity of organizational situations (local-global, individual-collective, practical-theoretical), organization theory sometimes takes on the appearance of a conceptual melting pot or frontier-free field of inquiry. Stakeholder theory accompanies this pluralist movement. There are clearly a number of tangible elective affinities between stakeholder theory and neo-institutional theory, and between the former and a large number of so-called political approaches to the organization, notably the coalition approach. Stakeholder theory is also inhabited by two powerful paradigms which emerged in organization theory in the 1990s: the social construct and organized action.

The Organization as Relation and as Organized But Unexpected Action

Stakeholder theory seems to express a dynamic conception of the organization. It does not cast the organizational entity, or at least does limit itself to doing so. In effect, the impact of stakeholders on the organization means that it is difficult to reify this last and present it as a finite entity with stable frontiers. Consequently, stakeholder theory has two notable paradigms corresponding to its own postulates.

Unexpected Organized Action   In Berger and Luckmann's *The Social Construction of Reality* (1966), a central place is accorded to action and "to context seen as the unachieved result of an ensemble of interacting phenomena" (Rouleau 2007: 164). The organization emerges from the complex interaction between pressure groups, the environment, and past factors (the identity of the organization, its beliefs, values and the ways in which it has resolved previous problems). The social contract model because it takes into account dialectical aspects existing in reality.

In this perspective, stakeholders do not determine the strategy of an organization by purely and simply attempting to push it in a particular direction. In fact, the stakeholders' projects are the result of the interactions between a complex constellation of phenomena which render the result random in that intentional action rarely produces the expected results, for the simple reason that action encompasses opposing external forces. Thus, results are explained neither by the composition of well identified groups nor by the characteristics of the environment.

The Organization as Relation   With the notions of interests and issues, stakeholder theory provides the organization with a multi-faceted representation of itself. The incentive-contribution model may suffice to describe the organization in relation to its stakeholders:

> "An organization is thus a system of interconnected social behaviors involving several categories of participants and stakeholders" (Desreumaux 2005). The organization's participants, personnel, partners, shareholders, directors, clients, suppliers, distributors, etc. receive advantages from the organization (salaries, products and services against the payment of a price, dividends or interest depending on the amount of capital invested) in line with their contributions. This representation combines two major issues that all organizations have to face: that of acquiring a knowledge of the useful functions of its members, and that of the skill with which the organization transforms contributions into products destined to generate anticipated profits. There is said to be a permanent tension between these two dimensions, a tension which is always negotiable: "we touch here on questions of coordination and the efficiency of the organization, both internally (the maximization of the output/input ratio and the minimization of conversion costs) and externally (seeking out the best negotiating position for obtaining inputs)" [Desreumaux 2005]. The always possible negotiation between knowledge about stakeholders' potential usefulness (proximate or distant) and the transformation of contributions into products encourages a representation of the organization encompassing a scale of action ranging from determinism to free will vis-à-vis its environment (Astley and Van de Ven 1983). Consequently, stakeholder theory orients organization studies toward strategy, regardless of whether the organization is considered as being governed by exogenous forces (a systemic/structural vision), modeled by deliberate and rational choices (a strategic vision), characterized by a continuous

process of adaptation (natural selection), or, lastly, as acting within the framework of a network (collective vision).

At any event, relations are not based on a knot of individual contracts or a relationship between two parties. The corporation is composed of an ensemble of individuals and of groups that have formed coalitions or which are in opposition to one another, but which nevertheless entertain contractual relations. In these relationships, it is not only the interests of individual parties, but also those of groups that are decisive. In this regard, stakeholder theory is different than agency theory (Jensen and Meckling 1976).

Organized Action as Sensemaking

One of the major contributions of Karl Weick's *Sensemaking in Organizations* (1995) is that it focuses on the organizational process rather than merely on the result produced by specific forms of organization. Thus, less emphasis is placed on real behaviors, events and structural determinants, and more attention is paid to meanings, more particularly equivocal meanings, "equivocacy being the multiplicity of meanings that can be given to a situation" (Rouleau 2007). Stakeholder theorists have been able to exploit Weick's paradigm, and the theory can be applied to an analysis of convergences and divergences between stakeholder interests.

Organized action is divided into three phases: enaction; the interpretation of the real and the attribution of meaning to it (sensemaking); and the retention of that meaning in the form of schemas which have become significant (organizational memory).

The stakeholders considered in a real or fictive situation are engaged in continuous processes in which meaning is created and diffused. In addition to the creation of meaning, diffusion processes include the act of influencing other people by communicating one's thoughts with a view to gaining their support. It is less uncertainty (incomplete information) than equivocality (multiple interpretations) which should be examined before action is taken. Stakeholders create a consonance vis-à-vis the multiple interpretations available to them. They attribute or impose meaning on objects, events and what happens to them. These meanings are applied when it comes to acting and understanding.

If the paradigms of social construct theory and of organized action are common to organization studies and stakeholder theory, the currents with which stakeholder theory shares most are, on the one hand, neo-institutionalism, and, on the other, the so-called political approach to organizations.

Other Currents Relevant to Stakeholder Theory

The Neo-Institutionalist Current

Stakeholder theory is in phase with what is generally referred to as the Third Institutionalism. While for the First Institutionalism, that of Philip Selznick (1957), an organization is different from an institution because it has to deal with its institutional environment, and for the Second Institutionalism, that of John W. Meyer and Brian Rowan (1977), an organization is the result of processes by which actions are constantly repeated, W.W. Powell and P. J DiMaggio's new institutionalism (1991) explains that, since organizations are open, they are faced with a series of different pressures (coercive, mimetic, normative), which mean that they often have to negotiate with or even conform to the demands of various external stakeholders. These three forms of pressure are placed in perspective by Meyer and Rowan (1977), who interpret the influence of rules, beliefs and rational myths professed as management rationality. It nevertheless remains that neo-institutional currents have been criticized on the grounds of their determinism (Westwood and Clegg 2003) and their shortcomings in terms of an over-emphasis on environmental structures and a resultant inability to properly take into account free will (Scott and Meyer 1994).

Political Approaches

"Political analysis is a generic expression for the ensemble of organizational analyses of the notion of power" (Rouleau 2007). It encompasses theoretical approaches from the 1960s, including the analysis of coalitions (Cyert and March 1963); the 1970s, including Crozier and Friedberg's strategic analysis; and the 1980s, including strategic contingency theories (Hickson et al. 1971; Pfeffer and Salancik 1978, 1981). Stakeholder theory is a major contribution to political approaches for which power is less an attribute than a relationship.

Coalition Theories and Theories of Strategic Contingency Three concepts are central to these currents, namely decision, rare resources, and interests. For Pfeffer and Salancik (1978), power within the organization is linked to a dependence on rare resources, which confer real or perceived influence. Pettigrew (1985) analyzes the way in which the interest groups of the British multinational, ICI, competed for control of resources and the processes by which change was legitimized.

For strategic contingency and coalition theorists, the organization is a system whose agents have such a large number of interests, which are so diverse, that its inherent conflicts threaten to cause chaos and eventually devour it (Hardy 1985; Narayan and Fahey 1982; Schwenk 1989). The first postulate of such theorists is that, since individuals have divergent interests, they employ agents to use their resources to influence decision-making processes, especially when they are either distant or excluded from them. The second postulate is that resources are rare (financial resources, information, expertise, access to decision-makers, networks, etc.) and that, consequently, potential for conflict is high. In these conditions, some decision-makers occupy a privileged position. In order to understand how actors use their resources to achieve their ends and influence decision-making processes, coalition analysts accord a central role to symbolic and legitimizing aspects of the processes by which power is mobilized. Such analyses demonstrate that the power sought by actors generally results from divergent interests. As Rouleau (2007) has pointed out, coalition analysis has also given rise to a range of studies on the phenomenon of the legitimization of power and the processes by which it is mobilized (Astley and Sachdeva 1984). However, coalition analysis treats managerial power and dominant coalitions as if they were sovereign within the context of the organization. Meanwhile, the political analyses of Hardy (1995, 2000) and Somech and Drach-Zahavy (2002) can be seen, on the one hand, as an attempt to reconcile analyses of power and strategic change, and, on the other, as an attempt to take into account the inter-organizational aspect of networks.

Conclusion

Compared to the multiplicity of analytical perspectives developed in the field of organization theory between 1980 and 2000, stakeholder theory is relatively unified. It has manifestly been linked to many currents of thought by dint of being contemporary to them or by having appropriated concepts associated with research in the field of organization studies. But systematic correspondences are still few and far between. It should nevertheless be noted that stakeholder theory is part of a trend promoting systemic analysis: it deconstructs the organization by focusing to a larger degree on a dynamic conception of organized action which produces meaning. Secondly, it enables researchers to more effectively analyze organizational, and more particularly, inter-organizational contexts which are increasingly international. It enriches the concept of the environment at the crossroads between strategic management and organization theory. In fact, the plethora of stakeholder maps including employees, clients and suppliers in the managerial literature and within companies themselves not only suffer from the drawback of not being applicable to all situations, but discourage interpretations of the concept of the stakeholder from the perspective of coalition analysis, strategic contingency theory, relational analysis, the analysis of the type of pressure deriving from stakeholders or being applied to them in view of achieving a result, analyses of the common good, and the framework of negotiation, etc. It should also be noted that stakeholder theory is linked to all currents of research focusing on factors of coordination (economics), convention (economic sociology), negotiation (international relations and political science), and theories of argumentation (rhetoric and political philosophy).

Chapter 4
Political Philosophy Interpellated by Stakeholder Theory

Because it articulates the existence of economic activities and agents in both society and the market, stakeholder theory is generally associated with a value-led approach to management, or, in other words, with business ethics. It is considered to have made a major contribution to corporate social responsibility. However, less interest has been taken in its contribution to social and political philosophy. This chapter examines how stakeholder theorists question contemporary political philosophy by focusing on its unresolved issues. In effect, questions such as the social contract, equality, and social justice are inherent to stakeholder theory. Consequently, the theory is applied beyond the sphere of its original management environment to question philosophical categories, while at the same time acknowledging the differences between one field and another. For stakeholder theory, the firm is the center; for political and social philosophy, the construction of public life, of the common good, of the art of living together has no center, and if one does in fact exist, it has nothing to do with economic life. This section examines the borders established between political, social and moral philosophy, on the one hand, and management science on the other; in it, an attempt is made to highlight the concept of "porosity" (Bonnafous-Boucher 2006).

The context in which the theory emerges is first envisaged in terms of the displacement of sovereignty between public and private organizations. Second, the issue of whether stakeholder theory suggests a new framework for analyzing civil society or, indeed, provides a substitute for the still operative Hegelian theory of civil society is addressed. Third, since stakeholder theory runs counter to the economic idea of a simple contract between individuals forming a pact defining a form of equality between parties who deal with each other on an equal footing, it can be said to propose a broader, more social vision of the contract: a social contract. Fourth, in the great liberal tradition, stakeholder theory adjudicates on the meaning of property and deals with the origin of equality, wealth distribution, and distributive justice.

© The Author(s) 2016
M. Bonnafous-Boucher, J.D. Rendtorff, *Stakeholder Theory*, SpringerBriefs in
Ethics, DOI 10.1007/978-3-319-44356-0_4

Conflict Between Institutions and Organizations

A new center of gravity, the corporation presents an alternative to public sovereignty in the form of economic sovereignty; thus, the equilibrium inherited from liberal philosophies of the eighteenth and nineteenth centuries, formerly based on an alliance between a public space organized and instituted by nation-states and a private space (exemplified by national civil societies of which corporations are a part) is breaking down. Stakeholder theory is accompanying changes in a landscape in which public and private arenas were previously distinct. Stakeholders represent a sort of globalized civil society engaging in a dialogue no longer primarily conducted with national public or parapublic institutions but, instead, with firms active in the global market. Up until now, the dual relationship between liberal democracies and capitalist systems of production has been based on a regulating exteriority, that of the rule of law, the guarantor of civil society's autonomy.

The gradual displacement of sovereignty's center of gravity poses the question of its legitimacy. Can multinational companies act as third parties? Can they arbitrate between stakeholders? These questions show that stakeholder theory is situated within a conflict of latent interests between organizations and institutions, and that it describes power relations between different organizations. As was mentioned above, numerous organizations of various kinds now compete with old institutions which once produced laws and norms and whose mission was to control the activities of private organizations. Voluntary agreements, notably charters describing commitments, translate this encroachment on prerogatives which were previously the exclusive domain of public institutions. This change of perspective expresses new needs within a framework of action in which, (1) the distinction between the national and the international is no longer meaningful (we act within an interior, globalized political sphere) (Beck 2005); and (2) the abolition of frontiers between the economy, politics and society marks the start of a new struggle between power and counter-power (Beck 2005) (Table 4.1).

From Civil Society to Stakeholder Society?

Stakeholders – the term covers a plethora of actors, individuals, groups, associations and firms – surely resemble the idea of civil society. The classical theory of civil society introduced by Adam Ferguson (1767) and, above all, by Hegel (1821) in his *Philosophy of Law*, defines society as all the intermediate groups between the two extremes represented by the individual and the state. Symmetrically, a stakeholder society would be made up of all the intermediary groups situated between the individual and the firm and, more particularly, major companies. Thus, while civil society is perceived in its relationship with the state, civil society made up of

Table 4.1 Understanding business ethics: an extended view of corporate citizenship

Corporate Citizenship

Social role of the corporation in administering citizenship rights

Social rights	corporation as provider
Civil rights	corporation as enabler
Political rights	corporation as channel

Source: Crane A, Matten D, *Business and Ethics,* Oxford University Press, 2007

stakeholders is perceived in its relationship with the corporation. The question is thus whether stakeholder theory can be presented as a new theory of civil society. However, an objection can be raised: while in the classical theory of civil society the state enables members of society to fulfill their potential for freedom, the corporation asserts its own freedom to function and develop without the freedom of stakeholders being a necessary precondition. Moreover, the corporation guarantees neither the rule of law nor the kind of pluralism necessary for a civil society.

The Hegelian Theory of Civil Society

By defining civil society as all the intermediary groups situated between the two extremes represented by the individual and the state, Hegel introduces a separation between the sphere of the organizing state (the political state) and the sphere of society (the external state), which includes the freedom of the individual separate from the state but linked to it by positive law and an awareness of the law. Later, Tocqueville asserted the autonomy of civil society: a vehicle for political expression, it exerts control over the state by means of its associative activism. Stakeholder theory reclaims the premises and developments of civil society by no longer basing the separation between organization and individuals on the state but, rather, on the corporation. For stakeholders to be able to form a civil society, such a society should be thought of as being built on an economic entity rather than in relation to, but independently from the nation-state, as in the liberal tradition. This change represents an important turning point in the history of liberalism and capitalism.

Three Factors of Correspondence Between Civil Society and Stakeholder Society

Recognizing Particular Interests The recognition of individual interests in the cornerstone of civil society. Civil society is characterized first and foremost by the egotistical tendencies of individuals who seek to satisfy their needs (§182). These individual interests are concrete, economic and social, for individuals in a modern society are dependent on collective economic production. Thus, civil society is a system of inter-dependencies between individuals in regard to the collective, "where the wellbeing of the individual depends on the standard of living of the entire community" (Fleischmann 1964). The descriptive approach to stakeholder theory develops the same hypothesis since each individual stakeholder represents a particular interest that has to be taken into account and the aggregation of individual interests can give rise to a kind of convergence (the convergent approach to stakeholder theory). The primary principle of civil society is similar to that of stakeholder theory in that, in both, individuals exclusively seek their personal wellbeing by means of satisfying their vital interests. But a superior common good is necessary to ensure that individual interests are able to co-exist; those interests are socially organized by means of work. Individual interests are linked to other, broader interests, which serve as means of achieving individual objectives. Satisfaction depends on the mediation of others.

An External State, Motor of a Liberal Society As a state external to the political state, civil society is the basis of individualistic, liberal society. "In effect, liberal society recognizes the rights of the individual to procure material goods, and recognizes as an objective right what the individual feels to be a duty, namely ensuring a decent standard of living for himself and his family" (Fleichmann 1964). Rights are identified with duties and the power of individualism is such that the notion of the common good seems no longer to have any relevance. As Hegel says, we are faced with a "moral reality lost in its extremes." Although the struggle between particular interests is justified (nothing universal can be achieved by simply suppressing the particular), it is nevertheless impossible to consider this playing field of interests as the ultimate objective of civil society. In reality, civil society exerts pressure and constraints on its members so that they are not merely individuals, but also useful members of a community based on the universal principle of work (§§186–187). Individual interest is neither indifferent nor abstract, and neither are individuals, who define themselves as belonging to a social category: for example, salaried industrial workers whose interests depend on their social situation. This is what prompted Hegel to write that "the family is the first precondition of the state, but class divisions are the second." In fact, civil society is accompanied by the emergence of a form of modern poverty which manifests itself as a mass of individuals (unemployed workers, peasants reduced to vagrancy, bankrupt artisans) who are literally *déclassés*, ejected from the class system (*Stande*), and who make up a paradoxical class (*Klasse*). If civil society is the mother of modern man, it is also an evil step-mother (§245). Its members become an aggregate of individualities deprived of the conditions which make it possible for free individuals to satisfy their legitimate private interests and their interests as members of a particular class through useful work. But if this were all it was, civil society would be no more than a "battlefield of individual private interests struggling the one against the other." It is here that we find the roots of the link by which personal interest is attached to the universal, or, in other words, to the state, whose task it is to ensure that this link is solid and long-lasting. Whatever the view of modern natural law, which confuses civil society with the state, individual interest is fundamental since the social contract, which is the genuine universal interest, cannot derive from an agreement between calculating, individual interests. Left to its own devices, the mechanism of the system of needs, the market, and production for and by the market transformed into class divisions, is likely to collapse.

The Universalization of Individual Interests Without positive law and public authority it would be impossible to pursue individual interests. Civil society perceives the gravity of the threat of the emergence of a state of nature within civilization, and develops a defensive strategy consisting of organizing individual interests within the corporation (in the French sense of the term). The corporation, or, in other words, the capacity to organize different individual interests, is the embryo of civil society. The corporation makes it possible for individual interests to emerge and organize themselves spontaneously, for example in the form of professional associations, consumer associations, etc. Partial interests are seen as always already social; they are linked to institutional regularities and regulations which keep interests at a distance by channeling them into external, relatively autonomous networks of solidarity. Civil society is thus a kind of external state.

In civil society, the task of the legal apparatus (Hegel 1820: §208) is to protect the common good – collective wealth, universal property – against the arbitrary actions of individuals. The law contents itself with maintaining the *de facto* situation created by the economic competitiveness of free men. The task of law, in civil society, is to protect private property. For Hegel, capitalism represents the conversion of private property into collective wealth owned by the entire community. And awareness of the law corresponds to civil society's awareness of the economic necessity of what it wants, or, in other words, of the universal goal by which it is motivated and which, in turn, it brings to fruition. Otherwise expressed, law and liberty exactly correspond to the extent that the laws necessary for the very existence of civil society are produced by the dynamic of the individual interests of which it is composed. Civil society is thus obliged by nothing other than itself to become aware of the law. But the process of external universalization which characterizes civil society is at once its strength and its weakness. It underpins the constitution of the universal concept of man as a rational subject with his own needs and interests, who is equal to all others in that he possesses the same degree of liberty (Hegel 1820: §190). This liberty defines the individual already determined as a legal and moral entity.

An examination of factors of correspondence between the classical theory of civil society and stakeholder theory reveals that of the three foundations of civil society, only the first strictly corresponds to stakeholder theory.

Partial Correspondence Between Civil Society and Stakeholder Society This examination of the classical theory of civil society demonstrates that while there are similarities between civil society and stakeholders, the two categories do not exactly correspond to one another. The old civil society is not reborn, Cassandra-like, in the form of stakeholders. Of course, like civil society, stakeholder theory recognizes the co-existence of an infinite number of individual interests. But the mere existence of those individual interests does not mean that stakeholders constitute civil society.

1. First objection. An initial objection can be made to the notion that civil society and stakeholders correspond to one another. In civil society, interests can be totalized in a universal (civil society itself), but divergences between interests can only be resolved by positive law (laws, courts) guaranteed by the rule of law. The descriptive approach to stakeholder theory does not totalize divergent interests within a framework encompassing them (even supposing a convergent theory of divergent interests): unless the indestructible character of all claims by all direct and indirect rights holders is recognized, stakeholders are mere aggregates. In this case, the intrinsic legitimacy of all stakeholders is legitimate, but it is not totalizable in a regulatory entity such as the state, complete with a positive law apparatus. The firm negotiates with stakeholders, but it governs without being able to totalize the divergent interests of consumers, suppliers, stakeholders and employees. It can only recognize and prioritize its actions in their regard: what does a supplier negotiating sale and purchase prices for his products with a purchasing director have in common with a consumer complaining about the quality of a product made by a supplier and sold by a distributor?
2. Second objection. Another objection is that stakeholder theory does not provide a mediating framework enabling stakeholders to express their intentions coherently, and, above all, collectively. Individual stakeholders express their intentions and rights, but corporate social responsibility is based more on incentives than on real legislation. In fact, the fragmentation of the law into regional jurisdictions prompted Powell and DiMaggio (1983) to conclude that firms apply a number of instrumental approaches to meeting stakeholder expectations. Firms conform to rules for the following reasons: because they are laid down by public and parapublic institutions (institutional constraints); because it is the law (coercive constraints); because professional authorities oblige them to do so (normative constraints); and, last, because they are imitating partner companies or competitors (mimetic constraints).

   In France, the law of 15th May, 2001 on new economic regulations made it obligatory, from 2003, for firms to publish annual reports concerning sustainable development (the annual reports of public companies include information about how they manage the social and environmental consequences of their activities). In the United Kingdom, a law passed in July 2000 states that social, environmental and ethical considerations must be respected in choices concerning which types of investment are to be made, how they are to be made, and over what period of time. However, in order to ensure that the legislation was respected, it was necessary to set up the Association of British Insurers in October 2001. In January 2002 in Germany, a law was passed on social, societal and environmental criteria in the running of private pensions funds. And in the Netherlands, pension funds have, since 2008, been legally obliged to invest 50% of their capital in CSR companies.

In July 2000, the UN published the *Global Compact*, a reference work in terms of respecting shareholder expectations, the aim of which was to define a framework for corporate social responsibility. In 1977, the International Labor Organization (ILO) published a tripartite declaration of principles on multinational companies and social policy. The declaration was revised in 2000. However, it is a question here of incentives rather than real laws. Nevertheless, although it is in the interest of companies to satisfy their stakeholders, it is not a vital necessity unless the firm takes on board the notion posited by stakeholder theory that it is dependent on certain relationships without which it could neither survive nor prosper. But the use of ratings systems, be they declarative or solicited, seems to be a normative method of constraint more effective than incentives.

3. Third objection. The intentions and interests of stakeholders are not manifested in specific categories, or what Hegel terms "classes." The very possibility of social categories raises substantial methodological questions. Thus, the identification of stakeholders is a recurrent problem for advocates of the theory. If we (1) precisely identify stakeholders influencing or being influenced by the activities of an organization; (2) or if we also take into account the embeddedness of the firm and, consequently, the way in which stakeholders are articulated between moral persons, public interests, individuals and groups of individuals; (3) if we discern the intentions of those parties; and (4) if we take into account the specific, historical framework in which the theory is deployed (an unusual type of capitalism, at once salaried and asset-based), then we will be able to describe the composition of the globalized stakeholder society and better understand how the firm deals with stakeholders it assimilates to a national or globalized civil society. The future of the theory, as well as its unity, is linked to its capacity to adjudicate on this third objection.

Stakeholder Theory and the Social Contract

The notion of a form of civil society based on stakeholders working in tandem with multinational companies rather than with the state should be placed, once again, in the context of 1980s America. Some authors have steered stakeholder theory in the direction of a theory of generalized agency (Hill and Jones 1992). From our point of view, stakeholder theory is dissimilar to agency theory because it attempts to build, from the foundations up, a social contract rather than a contract between individuals. The dominant current of the theory of the firm views social relations as if society were organized by means of transactions between individuals and institutions (Williamson 1985). This current is based on the sources of American liberalism described in the Declaration of Independence of 1776 which casts democracy as the fruit of a natural contract between individuals. The idea is relatively dissimilar to the social contract in that it presupposes that, (1) relationships are the primary form of social contract for which a legal contract is not required; in that, (2) the social contract is different from the kind of contract signed by two parties; and in that it stipulates, (3) an arbitrage between contracting parties or a guarantor of the social contract which does not have the same status as the contracting parties (particulars, members, individuals).

A Non-social Contract: The Firm as a Network of Contracts

The theory of the firm is associated with the institutional economics and transaction costs current (Williamson 1985; Aoki et al. 1990). It is dominated by a conception of the contract which militates against the possibility of a social contract in the full sense of the term. In institutional theory, the contract is a network of contracts struck between individuals and organizations (the salariat) or between organizations and other organizations (supplier-client relationships). Since all transactions involve costs (time, gleaning information on potential partners, etc.), opportunities for contracts are dependent on costs inherent in transactions. The lower the costs, the greater the pertinence of the contract. Williamson's major contribution is to postulate that the corporation (as an organization) is more economic in terms of transaction costs than the market, in which agents meet by chance in function of business opportunities. The organization-corporation thus possesses several advantages over the market: (1) thanks to its structure it has the capacity to draw up a contract and ensure that it is respected over the long-term, or, in other words, beyond a single transaction; (2) the *raison d'être* of such a structure is to minimize transaction and production costs (several transactions between partners can be carried out at one time). The advantage of the contract is that it defines the manner in which it is to be respected (although, of course, uncertainty regarding the behavior of the partners persists); (3) its essential advantage is that, although it is not possible to predict all possible outcomes and the kind of adaptations that will be required, the contract, at least to some degree, reduces uncertainty. In effect, opportunistic behaviors are always possible and conflicts can emerge over time. Even if it is contested by stakeholder theorists, this conception of the contract is an integral part of the approach in that it considers multinationals to be on an equal footing with stakeholders – free will to free will – with the two parties united by shared or divergent interests. It is as if a corporation were to strike contracts with a group or with isolated individuals. But a social contract cannot be based on an individualized civil law contract. For those interested in the plausible, non-fictive character of a social contract and in the contemporary foundations of such a contract, an analysis of the internal contradictions inherent in stakeholder theory is, in this regard, a necessary task.

Stakeholder Theory's Social Contract: An Alternative to the Theory of the Firm

The Propositions of Donaldson and Dunfee Between 1980 and the late 1990s a number of attempts were made to apply the notion of the social contract to the fields of management science and business ethics. In *Corporations and Morality* (1982) Donaldson sketched out the terms of an agreement between the firm and society. In the same year, Norman E. Bowie wrote a book entitled *Business Ethics* which examined the possibility of a social contract. In *La morale par l'accord*, Gauthier (1986) advanced the idea of a hypothetical agreement, the cornerstone of a collective morality based on individual economic interests. In 1988, Michael C. Keeley proposed "A Social Contract Theory of Organizations" which, while veering away from a strict interpretation of the social contract, presented a view of the corporation as "as series of contracts which serves as ways of reaching agreement about social rules."

From Contractual Agreement to the Social Contract The most successful transposition (and also the most faithful to the philosophies of the social contract) is that of Dunfee and Donaldson (Donaldson 1982, 1989; Dunfee 1991; Donaldson and Dunfee 1995, 1999). For the authors, the social contract is a kind of metaphorical glue – "ties that bind", according to the title of their book.

Like Rousseau and Locke, the authors regard the social contract as being supported by a form of pre-existing sociality. While the idea of a sociality existing before the contract is difficult to grasp, it is nevertheless the source of social theories of the contract. Faithful to the tradition of the contractualist philosophers of the Enlightenment, Donaldson and Dunfee present pre-contractual social relations as the basis and preliminary of the real contract, a kind of metaphorical "handshake" (1999). This notion enables the authors to highlight the fictive status of the contract: "If the contract were something other than a 'fiction,' it would be inadequate for the purpose at hand, namely revealing the moral foundations of productive organizations." It is useful to assume this fiction and the implicit agreement between stakeholders as the foundation of liberal societies: "The social contract is a powerful image which supports all forms of democratic government. In order for it to do so, we call upon a mythical agreement which provides legitimacy to a wide range of laws and institutions" (Axelrod 1986). In this vein, stakeholder theory "models" social contract theory and provides the pre-conditions for an agreement. Just as contractualists elaborate the ideal conditions of government in order to replace monarchy with a rational representative political system, in the business world some conditions are more equitable than others in terms of creating productive organizations and conducting trade. These more equitable conditions are expressed in a maxim: "Corporations should be able to do business, use natural resources and own shares, in exchange for which they should have ethical obligations toward all members of society" (Donaldson and Dunfee 1999). Thus, any profits taken should not outweigh the inconveniencies caused to members of society. However, it should be noted that the parties to the contract are rational, autonomous people who have given their consent freely and who have economic and political preferences. Donaldson and Dunfee even suggest that "hypernorms," or, in other words norms by which individuals are governed, make it possible to judge the actions of contracting parties. They apply the ideas of Charles Taylor (1989), for whom the greatest good is justice, and of Michael Walzer (1992), for whom there are nine basic criteria which render life in society possible, including the interdictions to kill, torture, oppress, and so on.

This initial level of sociality precedes the real social contract by which agreement is underpinned. However, some authors, like Kim Lane Scheppele (1993), do not believe that implicit consent is possible and question the likelihood of everyone having equal knowledge of and equal access to the financial markets (one thinks of the sub-prime market crisis of 2008).

The Integrative Theory of the Social Contract Donaldson and Dunfee have extended social contract theory to the corporation. Since "corporations are based on an ensemble of relationships and implicit moral obligations, this micro-social contract mirrors, at a smaller scale, involving fewer participants, the general social contract" (Cazal 2011). Distancing themselves from the both the classical social contract and the social contract as defined by Rawls, the authors have developed what they refer to as Integrative Social Contracts Theory (ISCT).

Integrative Social Contracts Theory juxtaposes the macro and micro levels. While the macro level reflects a hypothetical agreement between members of the community, the micro level bears witness to a real agreement between professions and/or trades and/or activities categorized into around forty different communities. This is how lobby groups are constituted with a view to developing ethical norms and principles for individual professions (lawyers, accountants), and how they are backed up by other political or economic networks (the European Community, the United States, federal states), industries (chemicals, software manufacturers), corporations (Canon, Microsoft, United Way of America), organizational units (human resources departments), and informal communities within organizations (networks of female managers, networks of Afro-American managers). There is no doubt that ISCT renders plausible a minimal level of agreement between individual interests which are, in many ways, divergent. It should nevertheless be observed that the institutional context of this social contract is very different from that of contractualist political philosophy in both its classical (Hobbes, Locke, Rousseau) and contemporary (Rawls) versions. It is informed by a crisis of the nation-state. A number of questions arise: will this kind of contract enable firms to form a "pact" with non-shareholders by creating a framework for dialogue and deliberation in which the expectations of non-shareholding stakeholders, who are subject to the activities of the firm, are taken into account and met? Donaldson and Dunfee's response to these questions is normative. They stipulate a kind of implicit contract between the corporation and society where the corporation has obligations to society which, in turn, has the right to monitor the corporation; however, they do not call into question stakeholders' capacity for arbitrage. In effect, Donaldson and Dunfee return to an idea of the social contract based on a more detailed description of society than the one proposed by stakeholder theory, which describes a more fragmented reality.

The Social Contract: From Rhetoric to Reality

Stakeholder theory offers a framework for reformulating the social contract. However, a number of objections can be raised in this regard.

The main objection is that, without a body tasked with regulating individual interests, there is a substantial risk that shareholders will lose all form of unity; unless a pact between stakeholders and corporations of the kind suggested by Argandona (1995) is implemented, the social contract is no more than a mirage. But let's, for a moment, imagine an extreme case of major risk in which the contract implies that impacts should be shared on a societal basis (large-scale pollution, for example). Let's also suppose that, on the one hand, there is an agreement between stakeholders, and, on the other, between stakeholders and the corporation. Who would be the legitimate arbiter in such a case? After many false starts, classical political philosophy opted for two solutions. One consists in an abnegation of decision-making powers in favor of a beneficiary third party (Hobbes); the other encourages the people to strike a contract with itself (Rousseau). The second solution guarantees the viability of the social contract based on the equal reciprocity of the partners. A pact is struck in which the collective, considered as an individual person, concludes a reciprocal agreement with all its individual members. This idea pre-supposes that the sovereign is "a collective, moral body" whose subjects are its members. Thus, "the social contract needs no other guarantor than the collective will, because harm can never come from individuals." (Rousseau: 1762a, V; 1762b, I, 7). In the absence of any common superior instance, the only guarantor of the commitment of the citizens to the collective is public force. "The fundamental pact tacitly includes this commitment, which alone can give strength to all the others, since whomsoever refuses to obey the general will, will be constrained to do so by the whole body." (Rousseau: 1771, I, 3; 1762b, I, 7). The result is identical to the one described by Hobbes's theory: the sovereign instance is the only judge of the execution of the contract and disposes of absolute power over all the members of the community.

Strangely, this notion is not to be found in any of the currents of stakeholder theory, nor does it feature in business ethics. The contractual proposition is a kind of "soft law" which does not constitute an alternative to neo-institutionalism. In effect, business ethics stipulates an implicit contract between the corporation and society; the corporation has obligations to society, which, in turn, has the right to monitor it. But it is as if business ethics were more concerned with being recognized than with the response to its demands. Such is the distinction affected between corporate social responsiveness and corporate social responsibility (Caroll 1979). Corporate social responsibility consists of "addressing one's obligations to society; it encompasses all categories of economic, legal, ethical and discretionary performance." Corporate social responsiveness, meanwhile, consists of "taking into consideration the fact that society makes certain demands which organizations have to meet" (Wartick and Cochran 1985). In the first case, the corporation shares values with stakeholders; in the second, the corporation is the receptacle of societal expectations. Evidently, the notion of a social contract encompasses both approaches.

The Relevance of the Social Contract to Stakeholder Theory

Because it highlights the origins of inequality in contemporary capitalism, stakeholder theory contains a form of social contract (which is not a contract between individuals) and attempts to establish principles of justice. The concretization of these principles is affected in an alternative model of corporate governance and through representative bodies seeking, among other things, to smooth out inequalities between owners and non-owners within the framework of the pure contractualist filiation of Rousseau's *Discourse on the Origin of Inequality* (1755), which prefigures *The Social Contract* (1762b).

Stakeholder theory deals with the distinction between those who hold shares and those who do not. From this distinction arise disparities that have never been resolved other than by a redistribution of profits from shareholders to non-shareholders who have either directly or indirectly contributed to the activities of the firm. The social contract hypothesis returns to the source of human inequality. The purpose of a social contract is to escape from the origins of inequality. Two hypotheses present themselves. The first corresponds to the idea of creating an equilibrium between the parties, or, in other words, between owners and non-owners. In this case, stakeholder theory focuses on extending shareholder rights to everyone. The second tolerates a constitutive inequality within society and a given mode of production if, and only if, that inequality does not prevent stakeholders from exercising their fundamental freedoms; if, in other words, that inequality is consonant with the idea of freedom as a primary, inalienable value, comparable to other societal values.

The first hypothesis corresponds to the idea of creating an equilibrium between stakeholders and shareholders by increasing the property rights of the former (Bonnafous-Boucher 2004; Bonnafous-Boucher and Porcher 2010). By applying the second hypothesis, termed "tolerated inequality," stakeholder theory highlights a disparity between shareholders (who take profits for themselves), and non-shareholders (who take no profits whatsoever but who are subjected to the activities of the firm and who often participate in them). This second hypothesis is directly linked to Rawls' second basic principle of "tolerated inequality," but the philosopher's responses to economic and financial disparities are only briefly evoked. The Rawlsian principle of equity is more concerned with the social than the economic circumstances of justice. In reality, socio-economic inequalities and the ways in which they could, potentially, be corrected are, essentially, considered in two circumstances, namely in conditions in which equitable equality of chance exists, and in the quest to ensure that the least well-off members of society receive the greatest benefit.

In the final analysis, stakeholder theory's major realistic contribution to political philosophy is to have risen to the challenge of a theory of justice by emphasizing the democratic instances of corporate governance. In sum, stakeholder theory seeks to establish an equality between shareholders and non-shareholders by encouraging shareholders to strike a balance between individual profit and the good of civil society as a whole.

Conclusion

Stakeholder theory examines the displacement of traditional sovereignties towards other forms of institutional legitimacy. Taking into account the upheavals of the institutional landscape, the theory requests that the global corporation contribute to the elaboration of the common good as the public good. This poses a major problem in terms of arbitrage and legitimacy, especially if, following certain authors, it is stipulated that corporate social responsibility provides the platform for a new kind of social contract.

From the perspective of stakeholder theory, the task of developing the common good is complicated by a major issue, namely the origins of inequality and the possibility of redistributing wealth (distributive justice) between shareholders and non-shareholders. Serious efforts are now being made to deal with this question by means of participative forms of corporate governance and its democratization.

Chapter 5
Stakeholder Theory and Ethics

Ethics: Justice, Equality and Fairness

With its normative underpinnings, stakeholder theory can be thought of as a philosophy of corporate or business ethics. Indeed, if we go back to its Scandinavian origins, to Rhenman and others in the 1960s, we find that the concept of the stakeholder has been subject to a constellation of normative and ethical questions. During this period, the idea developed that the notion of the stakeholder should be used to democratize business ethics, as the foundation stone of a more just and responsible corporate world. In the same way, the interest in corporate social responsibility mirrored the vision of the German unions of 1970–1980, with stakeholders participating in the management of the firm. Basically, business ethics has always been linked to the philosophy of stakeholder theory.

This normative and ethical approach to business gave rise to the theory of business ethics develops by Donaldson and Dunfee. However, as is demonstrated in this chapter, this is not the only way of linking business ethics to stakeholder theory. For example, business ethics can be considered from the point of view of the political philosophy of John Rawls. This perspective is not reducible to a description of the firm's stakeholders, but encompasses a reflection about the foundation of deliberation since it concerns a specific manner of choosing between different opinions held by the stakeholders themselves.

The Rawlsian perspective suggests an instrumental, strategic approach that elaborates an ethical theory justifying the use of a given strategy, while respecting the foundations of the theory. In effect, ethics determines the values supporting stakeholder theory strategy. It should be added that there is an intrinsic link between corporate social responsibility and the ethical model provided by stakeholder theory. This link presupposes the possibility of justice between stakeholders. We shall begin by discussing the main justifications for stakeholder theory before outlining a concrete version of this normative theory based on the notion of stakeholder responsibility developed by Robert Phillips and R. Edward Freeman. We shall then take a

© The Author(s) 2016
M. Bonnafous-Boucher, J.D. Rendtorff, *Stakeholder Theory*, SpringerBriefs in Ethics, DOI 10.1007/978-3-319-44356-0_5

Table 5.1 Clarkson's principles

Principle 1	Managers should acknowledge and actively monitor the concerns of all legitimate stakeholders, and should take their interests appropriately into account in decision-making and operations
Principle 2	Managers should listen to and openly communicate with stakeholders about their respective concerns and contributions, and about the risks that they assume because of their involvement with the corporation
Principle 3	Managers should adopt processes and modes of behavior that are sensitive to the concerns and capabilities of each shareholder constituency
Principle 4	Managers should recognize the interdependence of efforts and rewards among stakeholders, and should attempt to achieve a fair distribution of the benefits and burdens of corporate activity among them, taking into account their respective risks and vulnerabilities
Principle 5	Managers should work cooperatively with other entities, both public and private, to insure that risks and harms arising from corporate activities are minimized and, where they cannot be avoided, appropriately compensated
Principle 6	Managers should avoid altogether activities that might jeopardize inalienable human rights (e. g., the right to life) or give rise to risks which, if clearly understood, would be patently unacceptable to relevant stakeholders
Principle 7	Managers should acknowledge the potential conflicts between (a) their own role as corporate stakeholders, and (b) their legal and moral responsibilities for the interests of all stakeholders, and should address such conflicts through open communication, appropriate reporting and incentive systems and, where necessary, third party review

Source: Rendtorff (2009)

critical look at the limits of the notion of the stakeholder from the perspective of the philosophy of deconstruction developed by Jacques Derrida and Jean-Luc Nancy. A critical analysis of the foundations of the ethics of stakeholder theory demonstrates how the concept of the stakeholder community is based not only on the idea of justice and the notion of ideal communication, but also on the idea that the question of power and conflict can never be resolved in a normative stakeholder philosophy (Table 5.1).

Clarkson's principles are an illustration of a highly ethical and normative approach to stakeholder governance as a communicative, deliberative model of international management. The principles are as follows: "While multinational companies develop their activities and reciprocal links, managers and their critics seek principles of action that transcend national borders and cultural values; multinational companies attempt to develop a sustainable approach to achieving the firm's general objectives while avoiding conflicts associated with different human and social norms."

From the Ethics of Discussion to Deliberative Rationality

It can legitimately be considered that a vital part of the normative approach inherent in stakeholder theory derives from Jürgen Habermas's deliberative ethics of communication. In this perspective, all ideas are assessed in terms of their rational scope, and it is thanks to this scope and the ground that it covers that all partners in the dialogue can trust one another. The objective of dialogue, which is based on a democratic process of deliberation and discussion, is to create a consensus about the ends and objectives of the organization (Rendtorff 2009).

From a normative point of view, it would appear that the values of social dialogue are essential for promoting negotiation within organizations and guaranteeing equitable relations between stakeholders. In effect, dialogue between stakeholders goes beyond traditional dialogue with social groups still constituted for the most part by unions.

Negotiations between employers, unions and social groups are sometimes conflictual. But the way in which negotiation works differs widely from country to country, depending on legal traditions. Examples of different approaches include neomanagement, participative management, and employee driven innovation (Høyrup et al. 2012). Stakeholder theory introduces a change of emphasis from a focus on previously dominant institutional entities to entities previously thought of as secondary. In effect, stakeholder theory involves an integration of entities that are distant from the concrete life of the firm, ranging from bodies ruling on working conditions to decision-making bodies touching on corporate governance.

In the final analysis, the management rationality of stakeholder theory is a kind of deliberative, practical rationality in which discussions concerning management and governance invite the opinions of stakeholders, representatives of the general interest, rather than just individual interests.

The ethics of discussion and deliberative rationality introduce a concern with democratic principles within the organization to the degree that they are informed by a participative approach (Rendtorff 2009). Nevertheless, in terms of ethical principles, this ideal is not always respected. Examples of this include forced participation in dialogue and the ideological use of management-based values. In such circumstances, stakeholder theory is turned inside out, transformed into a disciplinary technique applied as a tool of legitimization (Fig. 5.1).

The Paradox of Stakeholders in Business Ethics

There are three models of the deliberative conception of stakeholder theory: Jensen (2001); Goodpaster (1991); and Solomon (1993; Bowie 1999; Ulrich 2008; and Rendtorff 2009).

For Jensen (2001), father of agency theory, the corporation has one, and only one objective, namely to create value for shareholders, which, in the end, creates value

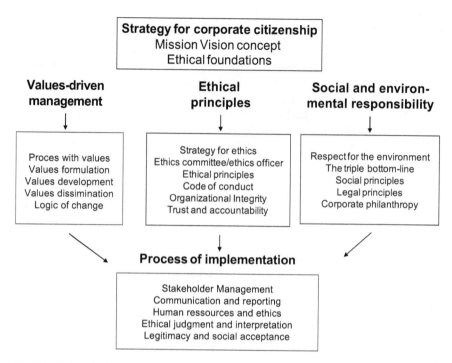

Fig. 5.1 Vision of ethical corporate management by stakeholders (*Source*: Rendtorff (2009))

for society. For the author, the objectives of shareholders and stakeholders are not mutually exclusive. The same kind of pragmatic approach is to be found in the work of the economist, Milton Friedman, whose position was similar to Jensen's, and who claimed that "the social responsibility of business is to increase its profits." The underlying meaning here is that there is a potential convergence between the interests of the shareholders and stakeholders of the firm (Wheeler and Sillanpää 1997: 33).

For Goodpaster, the pluralism inherent in stakeholder theory reveals a paradox – the "Goodpaster Paradox" – in that it encompasses the divergent interests of both shareholders and stakeholders. He resolves this paradox by stipulating the need to find a convergence between the interests of both parties. According to the author, the firm is a tool at the service of shareholders, which also has the obligation of serving the interests of stakeholders by means of an ethics of social responsibility.

R. Edward Freeman often highlights the pragmatic dimension of stakeholder theory, claiming that its objective is to find the best solution for everyone in spite of the different interests of the various stakeholders. From the point of view of long-term profit, stakeholder theory can be thought of as a pro-shareholder theory, since the emphasis on the needs of all stakeholders guarantees the organization's stability and survival.

Robert Solomon (1993), Norman Bowie (1999), Peter Ulrich (2008), and Jacob Dahl Rendtorff (2009) conceive of the firm of an organization whose ethical objective is to increase the wellbeing of both itself and the individual. When efficiency, rational care of the self, and strategy are based exclusively on individualism, they cannot guarantee, in the long-term, the economic growth of the corporation. These authors suggest an ethical and philosophical conception of the organization that is not located in an instrumental paradigm.

Stakeholder Theory and the Common Good: Contrasting Conceptions

Taking inspiration from Aristotle, Robert Solomon (1993) asserts that an organization that takes every stakeholder into account creates a shared existence and, thereby, renders possible the common good. The idea underpinning the common good is that it is possible to define a common objective, encompassing all interests in order to form a unified vision of the "good life" in the Aristotelian sense. From this point of view, stakeholder theory is a way of integrating such interests into a shared culture (Solomon 1993).

On the other hand, Norman Bowie (1999) argues in favor of an approach to stakeholder theory based on Kantian universalism. Reflecting on and organizing stakeholder communities is less important than thinking of them in terms of their global relations, or, in other words, in terms of the universal rights of all stakeholders. For Bowie, business ethics follows Kant's ethical principles, namely the categorical imperative, the foundation of the German philosopher's morality. An action is moral if it can be applied as a universal law and if it treats human beings as ends rather than means. The precondition of such an action is a respect of human dignity. The ideal of the moral law is the realm of ends in themselves (Bowie 1999). This position can be compared to the concept of corporate citizenship, which finds its roots in the Kantian and republican theory of the duties of the firm in society in regard to its stakeholders (Fig. 5.2).

From this point of view, stakeholder theory is evaluated according to rules of practical reason based on universal norms. The Kantian approach presupposes both a critique and a delimitation of the concept of the common good in the Aristotelian sense in that, for Kant, the idea of the "common good" can never be realized, since a consensus on what is livable is dependent on the views of discrete individuals.

Kant's approach to society is closely linked to the concept of deliberation and communication with stakeholders. In this context, attempts to structure deliberation according to the principles of the categorical imperative imply that actions must respect moral obligations and that moral law must underpin all decisions taken in the deliberation process. Stakeholders are considered as entities with their own dignity which must be respected as ends in themselves in terms of their existence in society. Bowie's Kantian perspective provides stakeholder theory with universalist foundations similar to those of the Habermasian ethics of discussion and

Fig. 5.2 Stakeholder management and corporate citizenship. The figure illustrates the close link between values, ethics and social responsibility in the strategic development of CSR (*Source*: Rendtorff (2009))

deliberation. This notion is foreign to the communitarian vision of the firm defined as an ensemble of stakeholders encompassing convergent and divergent interests both internally and with other, similar, group.

Directly linked to this Kantian conception, a republican perspective seeking to integrate ethics and stakeholder theory seems viable. This approach is based on the republican, or democratic ideal of citizenship as applied in the form of "good corporate citizenship" (Ulrich 2008; Rendtorff 2009). From this perspective, in societal terms, the firm not only has rights, but also obligations. Consequently, the legitimacy of the firm is determined by its ethical governance and the responsible management of its obligations.

Equity and Justice as Management Principles: Robert Phillips and John Rawls

In *Stakeholder Theory and Organizational Ethics* (2003b), Robert Phillips proposes an interpretation of stakeholder theory based on the moral and political theory of John Rawls (1971). The concept of justice as equity – or fairness – is the foundation of the notion of ideal, democratic and legitimate citizenship, a notion that can be applied to the economic sphere. From the point of view of economic activities, "ideal" means that citizenship of an organization is, first and foremost, to be understood in terms of care of the other rather than care of the self; in effect, applying the principles of social responsibility to oneself improves one's own competitiveness; "legitimate" means that the firm's behavior is moral and that it displays a degree of principle-based tolerance in regard to the range of values existing within it. However, "legitimate" does not imply displaying specific values (being a Christian or Muslim company, for example). In the final analysis, for there to be real legitimacy in the decision-making process, those taking part in it must follow a democratic procedure that encompasses all points of view (procedural morality v. substantial morality). The expression of such values is the manifestation of a life lived in common in a *Res Publica* (Phillips 2003b: 51).

The various ethical and normative approaches within stakeholder theory contribute to the elaboration of a framework of concrete principles underpinning the responsibility of the firm vis-à-vis its shareholders. "Company Stakeholder Responsibility" implies that ethics cannot be separated from the firm's other activities. This approach focuses not only on the instrumental, descriptive and normative aspects of the firm, but also, and above all, on its performance (Freeman and Velamuri 2006: 12).

Freeman and Velamuri propose ten principles of Company Stakeholder Responsibility. These principles describe an honest, pragmatic manner of promoting a social approach to corporate responsibility. They can be considered as tools for defining relations with stakeholders. The principles are outlined as follows:

1. Bring stakeholder interests together over time.
2. Recognize that stakeholders are real and complex people with names, faces and values.
3. Seek solutions to issues that satisfy multiple stakeholders simultaneously.
4. Engage in intensive communication and dialogue with stakeholders – not just those who are friendly.
5. Commit to a philosophy of voluntarism – manage stakeholder relationships yourself, rather than leaving it to government.
6. Generalize the marketing approach.
7. Never trade off the interests of one stakeholder versus another continuously over time.
8. Negotiate with primary and secondary stakeholders.
9. Constantly monitor and redesign processes to make them better serve stakeholders.
10. Act with purpose that fulfills commitments to stakeholders. Act with aspiration towards fulfilling your dreams and theirs (Freeman and Velamuri 2006: 7–9).

Freeman's principles of company stakeholder management allow for a thorough-going reappraisal of stakeholder theory. Instead of placing it in the center of the diagram (Fig. 5.3), the firm could, here, be conceived of as serving society and contributing to the common good. This conception of stakeholder theory can be represented in the diagram below (Fig. 5.3).

The concept of "fairness" developed by Phillips and Rawls can be applied in management because is it serves to support the procedural logic of the decision-making process. This approach is based on an equal respect for all parties con-cerned. In effect, what differentiates fairness from the pure principles of justice is the introduction of procedures for restoring equality while taking into account stakeholders who were not previously included in the dialogue (Phillips's "deriva-tive stakeholders"). It should be noted that Phillips develops a conception of justice that is neither simplistic nor egalitarian (2003a: 28). Fairness for stakeholders is

Fig. 5.3 Freeman's normative corporate stakeholder responsibility principles (*Source*: Rendtorff (2009))

more procedural than distributive. In this perspective, what counts is the democratic capacity of the economic activity and, more particularly, of the firm.

This procedural morality can be extended to organizations, even if, in Rawls's perspective, they are voluntary associations within society rather than fundamental structures of it. Phillips translates this vision of management by arguing that the individual is, first and foremost, a citizen, and only then a member of the voluntary association that is the firm. Consequently, although the association is voluntary, it has obligations to society, and these obligations are concerned, *de facto*, with the common good.

An equitable vision of the firm takes into account the situation of every one of its members from the point of view of their original position (Rawls). This means that, as in public life in general, potential members decide on whether or not to belong to organizations, with their decision based not on a desire to maximize their personal interest, but on their conception of the common good. In this perspective, fairness applied to stakeholder theory reverses the neoclassical conception of the firm: agreement about the public objectives takes precedence over agreement concerning its economic actions.

To the two concepts developed by Rawls (the voluntary association and the original position of members in society), should be added a third, namely that of difference. The difference between the members of a society or an organization constitutes *de facto* inequality: people are blind or they can see, born rich or poor, in an indebted post-industrial country or in an emerging economy. But the dependence of the concept of fairness on that of inequality is a paradox, since inequality is justifiable from the point of view of the weaker members of society, who can draw some benefit from it by finding more interesting employment or a better situation. In other words, for Rawls, inequality is, paradoxically, justifiable because it can be rectified: reducing inequality restores equality as fairness. Inequality is also legitimized if it leads to an increase in wellbeing.

According to Freeman and Rawls, at the heart of stakeholder theory is to be found a respect for the principle of difference. Respect for difference promotes fairness. This means not only that the organization should treat stakeholders fairly – stakeholders including shareholders, clients, suppliers, employees and public institutions –, but that this treatment of difference and inequality will help boost profits. In fact, respecting the principle of difference does not equate to a theoretical tolerance of all difference, but to the possibility of improving the fate of weaker members of society (Freeman 1993: 409–422) by taking their difference into account as, for example, in the case of conflicts of interest between shareholders and employees. From this point of view, it is a form of negative utilitarianism in which dealing with the inequality and difference of the weakest members of society takes precedence over addressing other forms of inequality and difference.

If the principle of fairness is extended to encompass relations with stakeholders external to the organization, it would seem that fair play is the most effective approach in terms of ensuring that actions in the market are just. The approach implies a virtuous respect for the rules of the game. Rawls derives the notion and practice of fair play from John Stuart Mill (Phillips 2003a: 86), defining it as a cooperative attitude to other people, the objective of which is to produce a virtuous circle of cooperation and responsibility. From this perspective, the notion of fair play is an ethical response to the risk of opportunism. According to Phillips, the notion, as developed by Rawls, is intended to generate "mutual benefit." Fair play implies that individuals limit their freedoms and respect the rules of a system of fair cooperation to the mutual benefit of all parties concerned.

Consequently, fairness includes a reciprocal obligation to ensure mutual profit. It is central to stakeholder management as the basis of business ethics and Corporate Social Responsibility (Table 5.2).

Based on the above observations, the following table provides a description of the various stages on the road to corporate citizenship. It is evident how demands on the firm grow as it gradually fosters a democratic idea of its relationship with stakeholders.

Table 5.2 Corporate citizenship

Level	Emphasis on strategy	Emphasis on activity	Emphasis on implementation
1	Corporate citizenship Elaborating strategy	Financing ethical missions	Making ethical judgments = mediating conflicts between ethical theories and principles
2	Developing the concept of institutional responsibility	Integrating individual and collective responsibility, constituting an internal ethical corporate decision-making procedure	Elaborating value-based management corporate ethics code programs. Developing corporate social responsibility policies
3	Developing a sustainable strategy of corporate development (*triple bottom-line*)	Engaging in dialogue with stakeholders Developing balanced scorecards and other tools	Communicating with stakeholders with a view to developing corporate citizenship (focusing on triple bottom-line management, reporting, transparent accounts)
4	Corporate governance based on CSR and stakeholder management	Integrating corporate social responsibility, business ethics and values-based management	Communicating with stakeholders about management principles, notably concerning the "good life" with and for other people in just institutions
5	Stakeholder management with a view to sustainable development	Promoting a *Purpose, Principle, and People* management approach	Integrating corporate citizenship and CSR through value-based management. Developing CSR and corporate citizenship accounting procedures
6	Developing value-based management in view of promoting corporate democracy	Developing a collective identity in view of promoting a respect for individual rights	Basing the identity of the organization on the principles of corporate citizenship

Source: Rendtorff (2009)

Deconstruction of the Paradigm of Justice and Ethics

John Rawls's ideal conception, a conception shared by a number of his commentators, including Robert Phillips, should be compared with a less irenic representation of justice. In effect, the tradition of business ethics often maintains a deafening silence about the tensions inherent in collective life, instead presenting the firm as a community of "friends" characterized by an ethos of cooperation. But, in reality, such communities are riven by opportunistic competitive behaviors: conflict and enmities are embedded in cooperation. The philosophy of deconstruction highlights the aporias and dilemmas of procedural morality and offers alternatives in terms of rethinking the very notions of the stakeholder, the community (and, therefore, the organization), democracy, and responsibility.

The concept of the stakeholder as interpreted by Phillips is a kind of metaphysics of justice. Now, in a deconstructivist perspective, stakeholders are defined by the very conflicts and interests by which they are animated; consequently, these conflicts and interests cannot be integrated into a metaphysics of justice. In this sense, Jean-Luc Nancy prefers to talk of an "inoperative community" which brings together independent individuals with heterogeneous, sometimes antagonistic values very different from the liberal society pictured by Rawls and Phillips. For these last, antagonisms can be resolved by means of a procedural rationality (social dialogue, representative instances) which lead to acceptable compromises (liberal social society). On the other hand, according to Nancy's concept of *désoeuvrement* or "inoperativeness" (Nancy 1986), the individual is always simultaneously inside and outside and, in consequence, always able to avoid compromise. A theory of the firm should be able to address the paradox of the tension between friend and enemy in reference to Derrida's *Politique de l'amitié* (1994).

For Jacques Derrida, a metaphysics of justice is impossible since justice is something that cannot be deconstructed (Derrida 1994). Justice is an idea of which all concrete manifestations are imperfect. Consequently, justice for stakeholders is impossible or, at best, possible only in a "community of the future" (Nancy 1986; Agamben 2011), since all so-called just decisions are exclusionary and there is always a party who has not been heard.

In the same way, the notion of the legitimacy of the firm is called into question on the grounds that it is a cosmetic metaphor that hides the power relations operating within a given society; while claiming to observe the rules of good citizenship, it simultaneously pursues its own private interests in the form of profit. From a deconstructivist point of view, the legitimacy of the firm masks the tension between personal interests and the public good.

Insofar as economic agents acting with a sense of fair play are concerned, the notion can be compared to "virtue," a traditional concept in moral philosophy reappraised by Derrida. The question is how does one go about, without duplicity, being at once competitive and fair when competition always presupposes the destruction of the other party? Poststructuralist philosophers are dubious about the possibility of fair play on resolving, on the one hand, conflicts between the firm and its stakeholders and, on the other, conflicts between stakeholders that can prompt them to say things like "we went to hell and back to win," implying that the victory was, in fact, a defeat.

Deconstruction calls into question the very idea of business ethics, which attempts to make possible justice of and in the organization. Poststructuralist philosophies insist on the irreducible character of power conflicts, singularities and differences.

Conclusion

In this chapter, we have discussed the ethical foundations of stakeholder theory. Our initial considerations focused on the way in which the theory goes beyond economic conceptions of the firm like those of Friedman and Jensen. Indeed, it also goes beyond a number of philosophical currents dealing with economic activity (including the firm), namely pragmatism, communitarianism, universalism and republicanism. In effect, these currents contribute to the development of a foundation for stakeholder theory by providing an alternative view of the activities of the firm. They focus on the possibility of the firm acting in the same way as an honest citizen. The approach, based on the philosophy of contract developed by Rawls, Freeman and Phillips has served as a framework with which to formalize this dominant perspective in stakeholder theory. However, dominant ideas about stakeholder theory and business ethics are called into question by a deconstructivist, poststructuralist critique. In our view, it is possible to found corporate citizenship on the philosophy of difference developed by Derrida, Nancy and Agamben. In fact, a stakeholder ethics presupposes the definition of a strategy based on this approach the aim of which is to ensure that the firm acts in a socially responsible manner, or, in other words, in the way in which a democratic, republican citizen would act in regard to the market and, more generally, within a democratic, republican political society.

General Conclusion

The essential objective of this book has been to gauge the scope of stakeholder theory in terms of its heuristic capacity.

The heuristic capacity of the theory enables it to achieve a level of generality encompassing the way in which the market and society are represented, while dealing exclusively which the representation of the corporation. Although a management theory, it possesses an interpretative capacity: it places the corporation at the center of its analysis by taking into account the porosity between the economy, society and politics (in the sense of "the polity," or living together). Stakeholder theory examines the frontiers between the activity of the firm and other social activities.

This heuristic potential has been addressed by means of an exclusively ethical approach to the theory. Readers coming to the end of the book might well ask themselves why the authors decided to leave their analysis of stakeholder theory's contribution to business ethics to the last chapter. The reason is that this is the most well known aspect of stakeholder theory, which is generally considered to be a mainstay of research into corporate social responsibility and business ethics (Anquetil 2011).

In sum, the task of analyzing the scope of the theory (and not only its state of the art) is still far from complete. In this regard, more room should be made for a constructive critique in that, as some authors (Acquier and Aggeri 2008), have observed, the concept of the "stakeholder" has become an ecumenical matter. And while the importance of a theory is often related to the number of commentaries it attracts, in the case of stakeholder theory, with a few, rare exceptions, commentators contributing to the academic and management literature are content merely to illustrate rather than critique. In this sense, the work of Orts and Strudler (2002, 2009), and Cazal (2011) provides a useful reference point. It can be demonstrated that:

- A sociological approach is required in order to make sense of a constellation of fragmented interests, with neither history nor context. This would make it possible to escape a holistic view of stakeholders in which employees and shareholders represent homogeneous groups; to better perceive coalitions struck

© The Author(s) 2016
M. Bonnafous-Boucher, J.D. Rendtorff, *Stakeholder Theory*, SpringerBriefs in Ethics, DOI 10.1007/978-3-319-44356-0

between stakeholders (Rowley 1997); and to take into account the American ethnocentrism of the theory, according to which society is made up of competing interests represented by lobbies.

- The theory is characterized by a kind of heliocentrism, with the corporation at the center of a model displaying direct dyadic relations between the corporation and its stakeholders. The literature is full of figures and illustrations highlighting this heliocentric approach. What has been described as a bicycle wheel could also be seen as a galaxy with the firm at its center. From this point of view, it could be asked whether the theory is an attempt to encourage the corporation to play a better role in society or an effort to teach it how to defend itself more effectively from counter-powers (Acquier and Aggeri 2008).
- Freeman's critique of the shareholder approach is reversible: the theory encourages the extension of shareholder powers to everyone (Bonnafous-Boucher 2004).
- The theory's normative postulates are problematic. In effect, the equality in law and fact of individual stakeholders (the intrinsic value of each one of them) makes it hard to justify a negotiation based on priorities which are not always those of the firm. In order to encourage a pluralist approach, it would be worthwhile comparing the arguments of Bowie, the major advocate of Kantian capitalism, with those of Mitchell, Agle and Wood, who promote the idea that stakeholders should be defined in terms of management priorities.
- Freeman's oft-repeated contention that he and his school subscribe to a basically pragmatic approach is counterbalanced by a kind of idealism apparent in his work. In effect, the idea of consensus, the cornerstone of the social contract, itself a founding institution of society, is bereft of tensions and of an exteriority guaranteeing individual freedoms. But stakeholder interests are egotistical interests. Thus, public organizations, public administrations, and political scientists should take a prudent approach to the notion of the stakeholder in that its origins are to be found in a representation of society in which the corporation is the basic social unit.

Certain authors, including Hatchuel and Segrestin (2012) maintain that stakeholder theory is incapable of "refounding the corporation," primarily because it is situated within the perspective of corporate governance. In effect, stakeholder theory is a theory of the corporation – more specifically a theory of the multinational company. It is, therefore, a local theory in that this type of company does not cover all forms of entrepreneurship. Nevertheless, the multinational is of particular interest, especially when one considers that, while in 1970 there were only 7000 such companies, in 2003 there were 64,000, with 870,000 subsidiaries employing over 55 million people. In many ways, the ownership structures and governance systems of listed companies reflect the profound transformations in the representations of capitalism mirrored in original theories of power and conceptions of corporate delegation and representation. But stakeholder theory is more than just a particular conception of corporate governance: it proposes a heterodox version of that conception. Indeed, it is also a theory of the value of the corporation. It has become almost a cliché in Europe to say that value is the result of cooperative action. In stakeholder theory, stakeholders represent this collective in their capacity as owners of interests, and although Hatchuel and Ségrestin (2012) deny that the theory is designed to foster or construct the collective, it nevertheless represents the corporation as the construction of a dynamic capability (Helfat et al. 2007). It affirms that, to exist and survive, the corporation and corporate governance must recognize and promote pluralism.

Last, the primary objective of this book has been to highlight the ways in which a management theory has been able to exert influence beyond its borders, a rarity in that management studies borrow more ideas than they propose. Second – and this is also a rarity – it is a management model that paints a critical picture of the corporation: the issues and interests of all those who are not shareholders or investors are primordial in terms of its survival beyond the mere ownership of capital. Third, we have focused primarily on the theory's heuristic function. In our view, this capacity can be exploited with a view to ensuring that the contributions of management science and management studies are more than strictly performative.

Bibliography

Abell, Derek F. 1980. *Defining the business: The starting point of strategic planning*. Englewood Cliffs: Prentice-Hall.

Ackerman, B., and A. Alstot. 1999. *The stakeholder society*. New Haven: Yale University Press.

Ackerman, B., and J.F. Fischkin. 2004. *Deliberation day*. New Haven: Yale University Press.

Ackoff, R. 1974. *Redesigning the future*. Hoboken: Wiley.

Ackoff, R. 1994. *The democratic corporation: A radical prescription for recreating corporate America and rediscovering success*. New York: Oxford University Press.

Acquier and Aggeri. 2008. « Une généalogie de la pensée managériale sur la RSE ». Revue française de la gestion 180(1): 131–157.

Agamben, G. 2011. *The kingdom and the glory. For a theological genealogy of economy and government*. Trans. Lorenzo Chiesa (with Matteo Mandarini). Stanford: Stanford University Press.

Aggeri, F. 2008. *Régénerer les cadres de la stratégie. Mise en dispositif et exploration de nouveaux espaces d'action stratégiques*. HDR thesis defended at the University of Paris, Dauphine.

Aglietta, M., and A. Reberioux. 2004. *La gouvernance ... autrement?* Paris: Albin Michel.

Ahlsted, L., and I. Jahnukainen. 1971. *Ytritysorganisaatio yhteisaiminnan ohausjaerjaerjestelmaenae*. Helsinki: Weilin and Goeoes.

Akrich, M. 1987. Comment décrire les objets techniques? *Techniques et Culture* 9: 49–67.

Alkhafaji, A.F. 1989. *A stakeholder approach to corporate governance. Managing in a dynamic environs*. New York: Quorum Books.

Andrews, K. 1971. *The concept of corporate strategy*. Homewood: Irwin.

Andriof, J., S. Waddock, B. Husted, and S.S. Rahman. 2002. *Unfolding stakeholder thinking*, vols. 1 and 2. Sheffield: Greenleaf Publishing.

Anquetil, A. 2011. *Éthique des affaires: Marché, règles et responsabilité*. Paris: Vrin.

Ansoff, I. 1979. *Strategic management*. London: Palgrave MacMillan.

Ansoff, I., and E. McDowell. 1984/1990. *Implanting Strategic Management*, 2nd ed. Englewood Cliffs: Prentice-Hall.

Aoki, M. 1984. *The cooperative game theory of the firm*. Oxford Oxfordshire/New York: Clarendon Press.

Aoki, M., B. Gustafson, and O. Williamson. 1990. *The firm as a nexus of treaties*. Thousand Oaks: Sage.

Argandona, A. 1995. *The ethical dimension of financial institutions and the market*. Berlin/New York: Springer.

Astley, W.G., and P.S. Sachdeva. 1984. Structural sources of intraorganizational power: A theoretical synthesis. *Academy of Management Review* 9(1): 104–113.

© The Author(s) 2016

M. Bonnafous-Boucher, J.D. Rendtorff, *Stakeholder Theory*, SpringerBriefs in Ethics, DOI 10.1007/978-3-319-44356-0

Astley, W.G., and A.H. Van de Ven. 1983. Central perspectives and debates in organization theory. *Administrative Science Quarterly* 28: 245–273.

Audier, S. 2012. *Néo-libéralisme, une archéologie intellectuelle*. Paris: Grasset.

Axelrod, R. 1986. An evolutionary approach to norms. *American Political Science Review* 80(4): 1095–1111.

Aymard-Duvernet, F. 2004. *Economie politique de l'entreprise*. Paris: La Decouverte.

Barnard, D. 1938. *The functions of the excecutive*. Cambridge, MA: Harvard University Press.

Barney, J.B. 1989. Assets, stocks and sustained competitive advantage. *Management Science* 35: 1511–1513.

Baron, D.P. 1995. *Business and its environment*. Englewood Cliffs: Prentice-Hall.

Baron, D.P. 2006. *A positive theory of moral management: Social pressure and corporate social performance*. Stanford University, Graduate School of Business Research Paper No. 1940, Rock Center for Corporate Governance, Working Paper No. 36.

Barnett, A. 1997. Towards stakeholder democracy. In *Stakeholder capitalism*, ed. G. Kelly, D. Kelly, and A. Gamble. London: MacMillan.

Beck, U. 2005. *Power in the global age: A new global political economy*. Cambridge: Polity Press.

Benseddik, F. 2006. Démoraliser la responsabilité sociale. In *Décider avec les parties prenantes. Approches d'une nouvelle théorie de la société civile*, eds. M. Bonnafous- Boucher and Y. Pesqueux, 91–105. Paris: La Découverte, Recherches.

Berger, P., and T. Luckmann. 1966. *The social construction of reality*. New York: Doubleday and Company. French edition by Armand Colin, 1996.

Berle, A., and G. Means. 1932. *The modern corporation and private property*. New York: Macmillan.

Bingham, J.B., J.R. Dyer, W.G. Smith, and G.L. Adams. 2010. A stakeholder identity orientation approach to corporate social performance in family firms. *Journal of Business Ethics* 99(4): 565–585.

Blair, J.P. 1995. *Local economic development: Analysis and practice*. Thousand Oaks: Sage.

Bonnafous-Boucher, M. 2004. Some philosophical issues in corporate governance: The role of property in stakeholder theory. *Corporate Governance Review* 5(2): 34–37.

Bonnafous-Boucher, M. 2006. From government to governance. In *Stakeholder theory: A European perspective*, ed. M. Bonnafous-Boucher and Y. Pesqueux. London: Palgrave.

Bonnafous-Boucher, M. 2011. *For a heuristic approach to management theory: Contributions to stakeholder theory*. Paper presented at the seminar held at the Center for Legal Studies and Business Ethics, Wharton Business School, April 2011.

Bonnafous-Boucher, M., and S. Porcher. 2010. Stakeholder theory and theory of civil society. *European Management Review* 7(4): 205–216.

Bowie, N.E. 1988a. The moral obligations of multinational corporations. In *Problems of international justice*, ed. S. Luper-Foy, 97–113. Boulder: Westview Press.

Bowie, N.E. 1988b. Fair markets. *Journal of Business Ethics* 7(1–2): 89–98.

Bowie, N.E. 1999. *Business ethics. A Kantian perspective*. Cambridge, MA: Basil Blackwell Publishers.

Brandenburger, A.M., and Nalebuff, B. 1995. The right game: Using game theory to shape strategy. *Harvard Business Review* (July–August), 57–71.

Brenner, S.N. 1993. The stakeholder theory of the firm and organizational decision-making. Some propositions and a model. In *Proceedings of the fourth annual meeting of the international association for business and society*, eds. J. Pasquero and D. Collins, 205–210. San Diego.

Brenner, S.N. 1995. Stakeholder theory of the firm. Its consistency with current management techniques. In *Understanding stakeholder thinking*, ed. J. Nasi, 75–96. Helskinki: LSR Julkaisut Oy.

Brunsson, N., and A. Goran. 2008. *Meta-organizations*. Northampton: Elgar Publishing USA.

Caby, J. 2003. Valeur partenariale ou actionnariale. In *Encyclopédie des ressources humaines*, ed. J. Allouche and I. Huault. Paris: Economica.

Callon, M. 1986. Some elements of a sociology of translation: Domestication of the scallops and the fishermen of St Brieuc Bay. In *Power, action and belief: A new sociology of knowledge*, ed. John Law, 196–233. London: Routledge and Keegan Paul.

Candela, J. 2006. Vers une notion intégrée de bonne gouvernance. In *Décider avec les parties prenantes*, eds. M. Bonnafous-Boucher and Y. Pesqueux. Paris: Editions La Découverte, Recherche series.

Caroll, A.B. 1979. A three-dimensional conceptual model of corporate performance. *Academy of Management Review* 4(4): 497–505.

Carroll, A.B. 1989. *Business and society. Ethics and stakeholder management*, 2nd ed. Cincinnat: South-Western.

Carroll, A.B. 1993. *Business and society. Ethics and stakeholder management*, 3rd ed. Cincinnati: South-Western.

Caroll, A.B., and A.K. Buchholtz. 2000. *Business and society. Ethics and stakeholder management*. Cincinnati: South-Western College Publishing.

Caroll, A., and J. Näsi. 1997. Understanding the stakeholder. Themes from a Finnish conference. *Business Ethics* 6(1): 45–51.

Casey, C. 2002. *Critical analysis of organizations. Theory, practice, revitalization*. Thousand Oaks: Sage Publications.

Cazal, D. 2011. RSE et Théorie des parties prenantes: les impasses du contrat, *Revue de la régulation*, Dossier: RSE, régulation et diversité du capitalisme 9, 1er semestre 2011.

Chabaud, D., J.-M. Glachant, C. Parthenay, and Y. Perez. 2008. *Les Grands auteurs en économie des organisations*. Paris: EMS Editions.

Chandler, A. 1962. *Strategy and structure: Chapters in the history of the American industrial enterprise*. Cambridge: MIT Press.

Charreaux, G. 1997. *Le gouvernement des entreprises: Corporate Governance, Théories et Faits*. Paris: Economica.

Charreaux, G., and P. Wirtz. 2006. *Gouvernance des entreprises, Nouvelles Perspectives*. Paris: Economica.

Chavagneux, C. 2004. *L'Economie politique internationale*. Paris: La Découverte.

Christopher, M., A. Payne, and D. Ballantyne. 1991. *Relationship marketing: Bringing quality, customer service and marketing together*. Oxford: Butterworth-Heineman.

Clarke, T. 1998. The stakeholder corporation. A business philosophy for the information age. *Long Range Planning* 31(2): 182–184.

Clarkson, M.B.E. 1995. A stakeholder framework for analyzing and evaluating corporate social performance. *Academy of Management Review* 20(1): 92–117.

Clarkson, M.B.E. (ed.). 1998. *The corporation and its stakeholders. Classic and contemporary readings*. Toronto: University of Toronto Press.

Clegg, S.R. 1979. *The theory of power and organization*. London: Routledge & Keegan Paul.

Clegg, S.R. 1981. Organization and control. *Administrative Science Quarterly* 26(4): 545–562.

Clegg, S.R. 1996. *Handbook of organization studies*. London: Sage.

Colla, E. 2011. Le concept de partie prenante dans la littérature en marketing: questions de recherche. Research seminar held at the Institute of Corporate Administration (IAE) at the University of Poitiers, Center for Management Research (CEREGE) and the Center for Research in Commerce (CRC) at Advancia-Negocia, Paris Chamber of Trade and Industry School of Commerce and Entrepreneurship, Aprel 2001, Poitiers, France.

Cornell, B., and A.C. Shapiro. 1987. Corporate stakeholders and corporate finance. *Financial Management* 16(1): 5–14.

Courty, G. 2006. *Les Groupes d'intérêt*. Paris: La Découverte, Repères.

Crane, A., and D. Matten. 2007. *Business ethics. Managing corporate citizenship and sustainability in the age of globalization*. New York: Oxford University Press.

Crozier, M., and E. Friedberg. 1977. *L'acteur et le système*. Paris: Seuil.

Cyert, R., and J. March. 1963. *A behavioral theory of the firm*. Englewood Cliffs: Prentice-Hall.

D'Aveni, R. 1994. *Hypercompetition: Managing the synamics of strategic maneuvering*. New York: Free Press.

D'Aveni, R. 2010. The age of temporary advantage. *Strategic Management Journal* 31(13): 1371–1385.

Derrida, J. 1994. *Politiques de l'amitié*. Paris: Gallimard.

Dery, J. 1996. Analyse bibliographique des écoles en stratégie. Actes de la journée Recherche en gestion. FNEGE Paris, October 11.

Desreumaux, A. 2004. Théorie néo-institutionnelle, management stratégique et dynamique des organisations. In *Institutions et gestion*, ed. I. Huault. Paris: Vuibert/FNEGE.

Desreumaux, A. 2005. *Théorie des organizations*, 2nd ed. Paris: Editions Management & Société.

Desreumaux, A., and P. Selznick. 2009. L'organization comme institution. In *Les Grands Auteurs en Management,* eds. S. Charreire Petit and I. Huault. Cormelles-le-Royal: Editions EMS.

Desreumaux, A.A., X. Lecocq, et V. Warnier. 2005, 2006. *Stratégie*. Harlow: Pearson Education.

Desreumaux, A., X. Lecocq, and V. Warnier. 2006. *Stratégie*. Paris: Pearson Education.

Dodd, E. 1932. For whom are corporate managers trustees? *Harvard Law Review* 45(7): 1145–1163.

Donaldson, T. 1982. *Corporations and morality*. Englewood Cliffs: Prentice Hall.

Donaldson, T. 1989. *The ethics of international business*. New York: Oxford University Press.

Donaldson, T., and T. Dunfee. 1995. Contractarian business ethics: Current status and next steps. *Business Ethics Quarterly* 5(2): 173–186.

Donaldson, T., and T. Dunfee. 1999. *Ties that bind. A social contracts approach to business ethics*. Boston: Harvard Business School Press.

Dondaldson, T., and L.E. Preston. 1995. The stakeholder theory of the corporation: Concepts, evidence, and implications. *Academy of Management Review* 20(1): 65–91.

Dunfee, T.W. 1991. Business ethics and extant social contracts. *Business Ethics Quarterly* 1(1): 23–51.

Dyer, J.H., and H. Singh. 1998. The relational view: Cooperative strategy and sources of interorganizational competitive advantage. *Academy of Management Review* 23(4): 660–679.

Evan, W.M., and R.E. Freeman. 1988. A stakeholder theory of the modern corporation: Kantian capitalism. In *Ethical theory and business*, ed. T.L. Beauchamp and N.E. Bowie, 97–106. Englewood Cliffs: Prentice-Hall.

Evan, W.M., and R.E. Freeman. 1990. Corporate governance: A stakeholder interpretation. *Journal of Behavioral Economics* 19: 337–359.

Evan, W.M., and R.E. Freeman. 1993. A stakeholder theory of the modern corporation: Kantian capitalism. In *Ethical theory and business*, ed. T.L. Beauchamp and N.E. Bowie. Englewood Cliffs: Prentice Hall.

Ferguson, A. 1996[1767]. *An essay on the history of civil society*. Cambridge: Cambridge Texts in the History of Political Thought.

Fisher, R., and W. Ury. 1981. *Comment réussir une négociation*. Paris: Seuil, 1982.

Fisher, R., and W. Ury. 1982. *Getting to yes. Negotiation agreement without giving in*. London: Hutchinson, 1981.

Fleischmann, E. 1964. *La philosophie politique de Hegel*. Paris: Plon.

Fleischmann, E. 1984. *Strategic management, a stakeholder approach*. Boston: Pitman Publishing Inc.

Freeman, R.E. 1981. Business ethics. In The state of the art, ed. R. Edward Freeman. Oxford: Oxford University Press.

Freeman, R.E. 1984. *Strategic management. A stakeholder approach*. Boston: Pitman Publishing.

Freeman, R.E. 1993. A stakeholder theory of the modern corporation: Kantian capitalism. In *Ethical theory and business*, ed. T.L. Beauchamp and N.E. Bowie. Englewood Cliffs: Prentice Hall.

Freeman, R.E. 1994. The politics of stakeholder theory: Some future directions. *Business Ethics Quarterly* 4(4): 409–422.

Freeman, R.E. 1999. Divergent stakeholder theory. *Academy of Management Review* 24(2): 233–236.

Freeman, R.E. 2010. *Stakeholder theory. The state of the art*. Cambridge: Cambridge University Press.

Freeman, R.E., and W. Evan. 1990. Corporate governance: A stakeholder interpretation. *Journal of Behavioral Economics* 19: 337–359.

Freeman, R.E., and J. Mcvea. 2001. A stakeholder approach to strategic management. In *The Blackwell handbook of strategic management*, ed. M.A. Hitt, R.E. Freeman, and J. Harrison, 189–207. Oxford: Basil Blackwel.

Freeman, R.E., and D.R. Gilbert. 1987. Managing stakeholder relationships. In *Business and society: Dimensions of conflict and cooperation*, ed. S.P. Sethi and C.M. Falbe, 397–423. Lexington: Lexington Books.

Freeman, R.E., and R.A. Phillips. 2002. Stakeholder theory. A libertarian defense. *Business Ethics Quarterly* 12(3): 331–349.

Freeman, R.E., and D. Reed. 1983. Stockholders and stakeholders: A new perspective on corporate governance. In *Corporate governance: A definitive exploration of the issues*, ed. C. Huizinga. Los Angeles: UCLA Extension Press.

Freeman, R.E., and S.J. Velamuri. 2006. A new approach to CSR: Company stakeholder responsibility. In *Corporate social responsibility: From aspiration to application*, eds. M. Morsing and A. Kakabadse, 9–23. Basingstoke/Hampshire: Palgrave MacMillan Houndsmills.

Freeman, R.E., J.S. Harrison, and A.C. Wicks. 2007. *Managing for stakeholders: Survival, reputation and success*. The Business Roundtable Institute for Corporate Ethics Series in Ethics andLead. New Haven: Yale University Press.

Freeman, R.E., J.S. Harrison, A.C. Wicks, B.L. Parma, and S. De Colle. 2010. *Stakeholder theory: The state of the art*. Cambridge: Cambridge University Press.

Gauthier, D. 1986. *Morals by agreement*. New York: Oxford University Press.

Gersick, G. 1991. Revolutionary change theories: A multilevel exploration of the punctuated equilibrium paradigm. *Academy of Management Review* 16: 10–36.

Gibson, K. 2000. The moral basis of stakeholder theory. *Journal of Business Ethics* 26(3): 245–257.

Gioia, D.A. 1986. The state of the art in organizational social cognition: A personal view. In *The thinking organization*, ed. H.P. Sims and D.A. Gioia, 336–356. San Francisco: Jossey-Bass.

Gioia, D. 1999. Practicability, paradigms, and problems in stakeholder theorizing. *Academy of Management Review* 24(2): 228–232.

Gioia, D.A., and E. Pitre. 1990. Multiparadigm perspectives on theory building. *Academy of Management Review* 15(4): 584–602.

Gomez, P.-Y., and H. Korine. 2009. *L'Entreprise dans la démocratie. Une théorie politique du gouvernement des entreprises*. Louvain-la-Neuve: De Boeck Université.

Goodpaster, K. 1991. Business ethics and stakeholder analysis. *Business Ethics Quarterly* 1: 53–73.

Granovetter, M. 1985. Economic action and social structure: The problem of embeddedness. *American Journal of Sociology* 91: 481–510.

Hafsi, T., and A.C. Martinet. 2007. The strategic decision-making process in state owned enterprises. *Gestion* 32(3): 88–98.

Hardy, C. 1985. The nature of unobtrusive power. *The Journal of Management Studies* 22(4): 384–399.

Hardy, C. 1995. Managing strategic change: Power, paralysis and perspective. *Advances in Strategic Management* 12: 3–31.

Hasenclever, A., P. Mayer, and V. Rittberger (eds.). 1983. *Theories of international regimes*. Cambridge: Cambridge University Press.

Hatchuel, A., and B. Segrestin. 2012. *Refonder l'entreprise*. Paris: Seuil, La République des Idées.

Hendry, J. 2001a. Missing the target: Normative stakeholder theory and the corporate governance debate. *Business Ethics Quarterly* 11(1): 159–176.

Hendry, J. 2001b. Economic contracts versus social relationships as a foundation for normative stakeholder theory. *Journal of Business Ethics* 10(3): 223–232.

Heath, J., and A. Potter. 2004. *The Rebel Sell. How the counterculture became consumer culture*. London: Capstone.

Hegel, G.W. 1820. *Elements of the philosophy of right*. Cambridge: Cambridge Texts in the History of Political Thought, 1991.

Helfat, C., S.W. Finkelstein, M. Mitchell, M. Peteraf, H. Singh, D. Teece, and S. Winter. 2007. *Dynamic capabilities: Understanding strategic change in organizations*. Malden: Blackwell Publishing.

Hickson, D.J., C.R. Hinings, C.A. Lee, R.E. Schneck, and J.M. Pennings. 1971. A strategic contingencies' theory of interorganizational power. *Administrative Science Quarterly* 16: 151–196.

Hill, C.W.L., and T.M. Jones. 1992. Stakeholder-agency theory. *Journal of Management Studies* 29(2): 131–154.

Hitt, C.W.L., R.E. Freeman, and J.S. Harrison. 2001. *The Blackwell handbook of strategic management*. Oxford: Blackwell.

Hofer, C.W., and D.E. Schendel. 1996. *Strategy formulation: Analytical concepts*. Saint-Paul: West Publishing.

Holt, D.B. 2002. Why do brands cause trouble? A dialectical theory of consumer culture and branding. *Journal of Consumer Research* 29: 70–90.

Hosseini, J.C., and S.N. Brenner. 1992. The stakeholder theory of the firm: A methodology to generate value matrix weights. *Business Ethics Quarterly* 2(2): 99–119.

Høyrup, S., M. Bonnafous-Boucher, C. Hasse, M. Lotz, and K. Moller. 2012. *Employee-driven innovation. A new approach*. Basingstoke: Palgrave MacMillan.

Hummels, H. 1998. Organizing ethics: A stakeholder debate. *Journal of Business Ethics* 17(13): 1403–1419.

Hutton, C.W.L. 1995. *The state we're in*. London: Jonathan Cape.

Huault, I. 2004. *Institutions et gestion*. Paris: Vuibert/FNEGE.

Jacquet, P., J. Pisani-Ferry, and L. Tubiana. 2002. *La Gouvernance Mondiale*. Paris: La Documentation française.

Jarniou, J. 1981. *L'entreprise comme système politique*. Paris: Presses universitaires de France.

Jensen, M.C. 2000. Value maximization and the corporate objective function. In *Breaking the code of change*, ed. M. Beer and N. Nohria, 37–58. Boston: Harvard Business School Press.

Jensen, M.C. 2001. Value maximization, stakeholder theory and the corporate objective function. *Business Ethics Quarterly* 12(2): 235–256.

Jensen, M.C., and W.H. Meckling. 1976. Theory of the firm: Management behavior, agency cost and ownership structure. *Journal of Financial Economics* 3(4): 305–360.

Jones, T.M. 1995. Instrumental stakeholder theory: A synthesis of ethics and economics. *Academy of Management Review* 20(2): 404–437.

Jones, T.M., and A.C. Wicks. 1999. Convergent stakeholder theory. *Academy of Management Review* 24(2): 206–221.

Keeley, M. 1998. *A social contract theory of organizations*. New York: Notre-Dame University Press.

Keohane, R.O., and J.S. Nye. 1977. *Power and interdependence: World politics in transition*. Boston: Little Brown.

Knox, S., and C. Gruar. 2007. The application of stakeholder theory to relationship marketing strategy. Development in a non-profit organization. *Journal of Business Ethics* 75: 115–135.

Kochan, T.A., and S.A. Rubinstein. 2000. Toward a stakeholder theory of the firm: The Saturn partnership. *Organization Science* 11(4): 367–386.

Kotler, P. 2005. *According to Kotler*. New York: AMACOM.

Krippendorf, E. 1973. Peace research and the industrial revolution. *Journal of Peace Research* 10(3): 185–201.

Langtry, B. 1994. Stakeholders and the moral responsibilities of business. *Business Ethics Quarterly* 4: 431–443.

Laplume, A.O., K. Sonpar, and R.A. Lits. 2008. Stakeholder theory: Reviewing a theory that moves us. *Journal of Management* 34(6): 1152–1189.

Laroche, H. 2007. *La querelle du contenu et du processus, les enjeux de la transformation du champ de la stratégie*. AIMS Montreal (working paper).

Latour, B. 1984. *Guerre et Paix, suivi de Irréductions*. Paris: Editions A. M. Métailié.

Laufer, H., and C. Paradeise. 1982. *Le Prince Bureaucrate*. Paris: Flammarion.

Learned, E.P., C.R. Christensen, K.R. Andrews, and W.D. Guth. 1965. *Business policy, text and cases*. Homewood: Irwin.

Lépineux, F. 2005. Stakeholder theory, society and social cohesion. *Corporate Governance* 5(2): 99–110.

Lussato, N. 1977. *Introduction critique aux theories d'organisation*. Paris: Bordas.

MacMillan, I.C. 1978. *Strategy formulation: Political concepts*. St. Paul: West.

Marchesnay, M. 2002. *Management stratégique*. Paris: Les Editions de l'ADREG.

Martinet, A.-C. 1984. *Management stratégique: Organisation et politique*. Paris/Londres: McGraw-Hill.

Martinet, A.-C. 1990. Épistémologie de la stratégie. In *Épistémologie et sciences de gestion*, ed. A.-C. Martinet et al. Paris: Economica.

Martinet, A.-C. 2006. Parties prenantes, management stratégique et politique. In eds. M. Bonnafous-Boucher and Y. Pesqueux. Paris: Editions La Découverte, Recherche.

Martinet, A.-C., and E. Reynaud. 2001. Shareholders, stakeholders et stratégie. *Revue Française de Gestion*, (November–December), 12–25.

Marcoux, A.M. 2000. Balancing act. In *Contemporary issues in business ethics*, ed. Desjardins J. R. et Mccall J. J. (dir.), 4e édition, 92–100. Wadsworth: Belmont.

Mercier, S. 2006. La théorie des parties prenantes: une synthèse de la littérature. In *Décider avec les parties prenantes,* eds. M. Bonnafous-Boucher and Y. Pesqueux. Paris: Editions La Découverte, Recherche series.

Meyer, J.W., and B. Rowan. 1977. Institutionalized organizations: Formal structure as myth and ceremony. *American Journal of Sociology* 83(2): 340–363.

Miller, R.L., and W.F. Lewis. 1991. A stakeholder approach to marketing management using the value exchange model. *European Journal of Marketing* 25(8): 55–68.

Mintzberg, H. 1979. *The structuring of organizations: A synthesis of the research*. Trans. 1982, *Structure et dynamique de organizations*. Paris: Editions d'Organisation.

Mintzberg, H. 1983. *Power in and around organizations*. Trans.: *Le Pouvoir dans les organizations*. Paris: Ed d'Organisation.

Mintzberg, H., B. Ahlstrand, and J. Lampel. 1998. *Strategy safari*. New York: The Free Press.

Mitchell, R.K., B.R. Agle, and D.S. Wood. 1997. Toward a theory of stakeholder identification and salience: Defining the principle of who and what really counts. *Academy of Management Review* 22(4): 853–866.

Moore, G. 1999. Tinged shareholder theory: Or what's so special about stakeholders? *Business Ethics: A European Review* 8(2): 117–127.

Nancy, J.-L. 1986. *La communauté désœuvrée*. Paris: Christian Bourgeois.

Narayan, V.K., and L. Fahey. 1982. The micro-politics of strategy formulation. *Academy of Management Review* 7(1): 25–34.

Näsi, J. 1995. What is stakeholder thinking? A snapshot of a social theory of the firm. In *Understanding stakeholder thinking*, ed. J. Näsi, 19–32. Helsinki: LSR-Julkaisut Oy.

Nicolini, D., S. Gherardi, and D. Yanow. 2003. Introduction: Toward a practice-based view of knowing and learning in organizations. In *Knowing in organizations. A practice-based approach*, ed. D. Nicolini, S. Gherardi, and D. Yanow, 3–31. London: Sharpe.

Orts, E.W., and A. Strudler. 2002. The ethical and environmental limits of stakeholder theory. *Business Ethics Quaterly* 12(2): 215–234.

Orts, E.W., and A. Strudler. 2009. Putting a stake in stakeholder theory. *Business Ethics Quarterly* 88: 605–615.

Parrat, F. 1999. *Le gouvernement d'entreprise: ce qui a changé, ce qui va évoluer*. Paris: Maxime L. du Mesnil.

Pasquero, J. 1980. *L'entreprise face aux pressions sociopolitiques de son environnement*. PhD thesis, Université des sciences sociales de Grenoble, IAE.

Pasquero, J. 2008. Entreprise, Développement durable et Théorie des parties prenantes: esquisse d'un arrimage socio-constructionniste. *Management International* 12: 27–47.

Penrose, E. 1959. *The theory of the growth of the firm*. Oxford: Blackwell.

Perez, R. 2003. *La gouvernance de l'entreprise*. Paris: La Découverte.

Pettigrew, A.M. 1985. *The awakening giant*. Oxford: Blackwell.

Pfeffer, J., and G.R. Salancik. 1978. *The external control of organization: A resource dependence perspective*. New York: Harper and Row.

Pfeffer, J., and G.R. Salancik. 1981. *Power in organizations*. Marshfield: Pitman.

Phillips, R. 2003a. Stakeholder legitimacy. *Business Ethics Quarterly* 13: 25–41.

Phillips, R. 2003b. *Stakeholder theory and organizational ethics*. San Francisco: Berrett-Koehler, Inc.

Phillips, R., and R.E. Freeman. 2010. *Stakeholders*. Cheltenham: Edward Elgar.

Phillips, A., and J. Reichart. 2000. The environment as a stakeholder? A fairness-based approach. *Journal of Business Ethics* 23: 185–197.

Phillips, R., R.E. Freeman, and A.C. Wicks. 2003. What stakeholder theory is not. *Business Ethics Quarrterly* 13(4): 479–502.

Polanyi, K. 1944. *The great transformation*. New York: Farrar and Rinehart.

Porter, M. 1980. *Competitive strategy*. New York: The Free Press.

Porter, M. 1985. *Competitive advantage*. New York: The Free Press.

Porter, M., and M. Kramer. 2002. The competitive advantage of corporate philanthropy. *Harvard Business Review* 80(12): 56–68.

Porter, M., and M. Kramer. 2011. Creating shared value. How to reinvent capitalism – and unleash a wave of innovation and growth. *Harvard Business Review* 89(1/2): 62–77.

Post, J.E., L.E. Preston, and S. Sachs. 2002. *Redefining the corporation, stakeholder management and organizational wealth*. Stanford: Stanford University Press.

Powell, W.W., and P.J. DiMaggio. 1983. The iron cage revisited: Functional isomorphism and collective rationality in organizational fields. *American Journal of Sociology* 48(2): 147–160.

Powell, W.W., and P.J. DiMaggio (eds.). 1991. *The new institutionalism in organizational analysis*. Chicago: University of Chicago Press.

Preston, L.E., and J.E. Post. 1975. *Private management and public choice: The principle of public responsibility*. Englewood Cliffs: Prentice-Hall.

Rawls, J. 1971. *A theory of justice*. Cambridge: Harvard University Press.

Rendtorff Dahl, J. 2009. *Responsibility, ethics and legitimacy of corporations*. Copenhagen: Copenhagen Business School Press.

Rhenman, E., and B. Stymne. 1965. *Företagsledning i en föränderlig värld*. Stockholm: Aldus/Bonniers.

Robbins, S.P. 1987. *Organization theory*. Englewood Cliffs: Prenctice-Hall.

Roper, S., and G. Davies. 2007. The corporate brand: Dealing with multiple stakeholders. *Journal of Marketing Management* 23(1–2): 75–90.

Rouleau, L. 2007. *Théories des Organisations, Approches classiques, contemporaines et de l'avant-garde*. Quebec City: Presses de l'université du Québec.

Rousseau, J.-J. 1762a. *Émile ou De l'éducation*. In *Œuvres complètes* IV. Paris: La Pléiade.

Rousseau, J.-J. 1762b. *Du contrat social ou Essai sur la forme de la république*. In *Œuvres complètes* III. Paris: La Pléiade.

Rousseau, J.-J. 1771. *Manuscrit de Genève*. In *Œuvres complètes* III. Paris: La Pléiade.

Rousseau, J.-J. 1775. *Discours sur l'origine de l'inégalité parmi les hommes*. In *Œuvres complètes* III. Paris: La Pléiade.

Roux, D. 2007. La résistance du consommateur. Proposition d'un cadre d'analyse. *Recherche et Applications en Marketing* 22(4): 59–80.

Rowley, L. 1997. Moving beyond dyadic ties: A network theory of stakeholder influences. *Academy of Management Review* 22(4): 887–910.

Rustin, M. 1997. Stakeholding and the public sector. In *Stakeholder capitalism*, ed. G. Kelly, D. Kelly, and A. Gamble. London: MacMillan.

Sachs, S., and E. Ruhli. 2011. *Stakeholders matter. A new paradigm for strategy in society*. Cambridge: Cambridge University Press.

Savage, G.T., T.H. Nix, C.J. Whitehead, and J.D. Blair. 1991. Strategies for assessing and managing organizational stakeholders. *Academy of Management Executive* 5(2): 61–75.

Scheppele, K.L. 1993. It's just not right: The ethics of insider trading. *Law and Contemporary Problems* 56(3): 123–173.

Schwenk, C.R. 1989. Linking cognition, organizational and political factors in exploring strategic change. *Journal of Management Studies* 26(2): 177–187.

Scott, R.W. 1987. *Organizations, rational, natural and open systems*. Englewood Cliffs: Prentice-Hall.

Scott, R.W. 1995. *Institutions and organizations*. Thousand Oaks: Sage.

Scott, R.W., and J.W. Meyer. 1994. *Institutional environments and organizations: Structural complexity and individualism*. Thousand Oaks: Sage.

Schleifer, A., and R.W. Vishnhy. 1997, Jun. A survey of corporate governance. *The Journal of Finance* 52(2): 737–783.

Selznick, P. 1957. *Leadership in administration*. New York: Harper and Row.

Senghaas, D. 1973. Conflict formations in contemporary international society. *Journal of Peace Research* 10(3): 163–184.

Smith, A. 1982[1759]. In *The theory of moral sentiments*, eds. D.D. Raphael and A.L. Macfie. London: Liberty Fund.

Solomon, R.C. 1993. *Ethics and excellence. Cooperation and integrity in business*. Oxford: Oxford University Press.

Somech, A., and A. Drach-Zahavy. 2002. Relative power and influence strategy: The effects of agent/target organizational power on superiors' choices of influence strategies. *Journal of Organizational Behavior* 23(2): 167–178.

Stanford Research Institute. 1963. *Internal Memorandum*. Stanford.

Starik, M. 1994. *Essays by Mark Starik*. Toronto conference: Reflections on Stakeholder Theory. *Business and Society* 33:82–131.

Sternberg, E. 2000. *Just business*. New York: Oxford University Press.

Stewart, G.B. 1994. EVA: Fact and fantasy. *Journal of Applied Corporate Finance* 7(2): 71–84.

Strati, A. 1999. *Organization and aesthetics*. Thousand Oaks: Sage.

Susskind, L. 2000. *The consensus building handbook*. Thousand Oaks: Sage.

Tabatoni, P., and P. Jarniou. 1975. *Les systèmes de gestion: politiques et structures*. Paris: PUF.

Taylor, C. 1989. *Sources of the self*. Cambridge, MA: Harvard University Press.

Thomson, J.K., S.L. Wartick, and H.L. Smith. 1991. Integrating corporate social performance and stakeholder management: Implication for a research agenda in small business. *Research in Corporate Social Performance and Policy* 12: 207–230.

Thuderoz, C. 2010. *Qu'est-ce que négocier? Sociologie du compromis et de l'action*. Rennes: Presses universitaires de Rennes.

Tichy, N.M., A.R. McGill, and L. Saint-Clair. 1997. *Corporate global citizenship, doing business in the public eye*. San Francisco: The New Lexington Press.

Tsoukas, H., and C. Knudsen. 2003. *The Oxford handbook of organization theory*. Oxford: Oxford University Press.

Ulrich, P. 2008. *Integrative economic ethics: Foundations of a civilized market economy*. Cambridge: Cambridge University Press.

van Buren, H.J. 2001. If fairness is the problem, is consent the solution? Integrating ISCT and stakeholder theory. *Business Ethics Quarterly* 11(3): 481–499.

Venkataraman, S. 2002. Stakeholder value equilibration and the entrepreneurial process. In *Ethics and entrepreneurship*, eds. R.E. Freeman and S. Venkataraman, 45–57. Charlottesville: Ruffin Series, Philosophy Documentation Center.

von Bertalanffy, Ludwig. 1951. General system theory. A new approach to unity of science (symposium). *Human Biology* 23: 303–361.

von Bertalanffy, Ludwig. 1968. *General system theory: Foundations, development, applications*. New York: George Braziller.

Walzer, M. 1992. Moral minimalism. In *The Twilight of probability: Ethics and politics*, ed. W.R. Shea and G.A. Spadafora, 3–14. Canton: Science History Publications.

Wartick, S.L., and P.L. Cochran. 1985. The evolution of the corporate social performance model. *Academy of Management Review* 10(4): 758–769.

Weick, K. 1995. *Sensemaking in organizations*. Thousand Oaks: Sage.

Wernerfelt, B. 1984. A resource-based view of the firm. *Strategic Management Journal* 5(2) (April–June): 171–180.

Westwood, R., and S.R. Clegg. 2003. The problem of order revisited: Towards a more critical institutional perspective. *Debating Organization.* Oxford: Blackwell.

Wheeler, D., and M. Sillanpää. 1997. *The stakeholder corporation. The body shop blue print for maximizing stakeholder value.* London: Pitman Publishing.

Wicks, A.C., and T.M. Jones. 1999. Convergent stakeholder theory. *Academy of Management Review* 24(2): 206–221.

Wicks, A., R.E. Freeman, and P.H. Werhane. 2009. *Business ethics: A managerial approach.* Englewood Cliffs: Prentice-Hall.

Wicks, A.C., D.R. Gilbert, and R.E. Freeman. 1994. A feminist reinterpretation of the stakeholder concept. *Business Ethics Quarterly* 4(4): 475–497.

Williamson, O. 1985. *The economic institutions of capitalism.* New York: The Free Press.

Wirtz, P. 2008. *Les meilleures pratiques de gouvernance d'entreprise.* Paris: La Découverte, Repères.

CPSIA information can be obtained
at www.ICGtesting.com
Printed in the USA
LVHW011910280821
696355LV00005B/298